Civil Service Exam Made Easy

Insider Secrets for First-Time Success | 510 Practice Q&A, Explanations and Digital Flashcards

Lucas Males

Publishing Help

TABLE OF CONTENTS

CHAPTER 1

INTRODUCTION TO THE CIVIL SERVICE EXAM

Understanding the Civil Service System

Civil service exams have long been a gateway to a career in public service, offering individuals the opportunity to contribute meaningfully to society. These exams serve as a standardized method to assess candidates' suitability for roles within various government sectors. Understanding the civil service system is crucial for anyone considering a career in this field, as it forms the foundation for the entire examination process.

The civil service system is designed to ensure that government positions are filled based on merit rather than connections or personal influence. This merit-based approach aims to maintain fairness, equality, and transparency in the recruitment process. It is a testament to the principle that every candidate should have an equal chance to serve the public, regardless of their background or affiliations.

At the heart of the civil service system lies the classification of different types of exams. These exams can vary significantly depending on the role, the level of government, and the specific requirements of the position. Broadly, civil service exams can be categorized into federal, state, and municipal exams. Each level of government has its own set of criteria and processes, but the underlying goal remains the same: to select the most qualified individuals for public service roles.

Federal civil service exams are typically designed for positions within national government agencies. These exams often test a wide range of skills, from analytical abilities to subject-specific knowledge. Candidates may be required to demonstrate proficiency in areas such as law, finance, or public administration, depending on the job's nature. Federal exams are usually comprehensive and may include both written and oral components to thoroughly assess a candidate's capabilities.

State civil service exams, on the other hand, are tailored to the needs of state government positions. While they share similarities with federal exams, they often focus more on state-specific legislation, policies, and procedures. These exams are essential for roles that require a deep understanding of state governance and public sector operations. Like federal exams, state exams can include a combination of written tests, interviews, and practical assessments.

Municipal civil service exams are designed for positions within local government entities, such as city or county offices. These exams often emphasize skills relevant to the community, such as customer service, clerical tasks, and public safety. Municipal exams provide an entry point for individuals looking to make a direct impact on their local communities. The exam content is usually tailored to the specific functions and responsibilities of the local government roles.

The importance of civil service exams extends beyond the selection process. They act as a benchmark for evaluating the competencies and potential of candidates, ensuring that those who enter public service are equipped to handle the responsibilities of their positions. This is particularly significant in roles that involve critical decision-making, public safety, or the management of public resources.

Despite their critical role in the recruitment process, civil service exams are often surrounded by myths and misconceptions. One common myth is that these exams are insurmountably difficult, deterring many potential candidates from even attempting to take them. While it is true that civil service exams can be challenging, they are not designed to be impossible. With the right preparation and understanding, candidates can navigate these exams successfully.

Another misconception is that passing a civil service exam guarantees immediate employment. In reality, passing the exam is just one step in the hiring process. Candidates may still need to undergo interviews, background checks, and other evaluations before being offered a position. It is important for candidates to recognize that success in the exam is part of a larger journey towards a career in public service.

A merit-based system like the civil service is also often misunderstood. Some individuals believe that connections and influence can still play a role in the hiring process. While no system is entirely immune to human biases, the civil service system is structured to minimize such influences. The exams are standardized, and the selection criteria are clearly defined to ensure that all candidates are evaluated equally.

Understanding these aspects of the civil service system is essential for anyone preparing to take a civil service exam. It helps candidates approach the exam with the right mindset, armed with the knowledge that their success depends on their own abilities and efforts. Moreover, it emphasizes the importance of preparation, as candidates must be well-versed in both the content of the exam and the processes that follow.

Types of Civil Service Exams

Civil service exams serve as a vital gateway for individuals aspiring to join the ranks of public service. These exams are carefully designed to evaluate the knowledge, skills, and abilities of candidates, ensuring that only the most qualified individuals fill crucial roles in government. Understanding the different types of civil service exams is essential for anyone preparing to embark on this journey, as it helps tailor preparation strategies to specific exam formats and requirements.

The diversity in civil service exams reflects the wide range of roles available within government sectors. Each type of exam is tailored to assess the competencies required for specific positions, whether they be administrative, technical, or managerial. At the federal level, exams are generally comprehensive, covering a broad spectrum of skills and knowledge areas. Federal exams tend to be more standardized across the board, often testing candidates on general competencies like analytical skills, problem-solving abilities, and subject-specific knowledge. These exams might also include components that assess a candidate's understanding of federal laws, policies, and procedures, given the national scope of the roles they're being considered for.

State-level civil service exams, on the other hand, are crafted with the unique needs of state government positions in mind. While they share some similarities with federal exams in terms of structure, they often emphasize state-specific legislation and policies. These exams may cover topics such as local governance, state regulations, and region-specific issues. The focus is on ensuring that candidates are well-versed in the nuances of state operations, as these roles often require a deep understanding of the state's legislative framework and administrative practices.

Municipal civil service exams are specifically designed for positions within city or county government entities. These exams often prioritize skills relevant to local governance and community services. As municipal roles can vary widely—from clerical positions to law enforcement—the exams are tailored to assess the specific requirements of each role. For instance, a civil service exam for a police officer position may include physical fitness tests, psychological evaluations, and assessments of legal knowledge, whereas an exam for a clerical role may focus more on administrative skills, customer service abilities, and clerical proficiency.

One of the key distinctions among these exams is the level of specialization required. Some civil service exams are highly specialized, targeting particular fields such as engineering, healthcare, or information technology. These exams require candidates to demonstrate expertise in their chosen field, often through technical questions and practical assessments. Specialized exams are common in positions where technical skills and professional qualifications are critical to job performance.

In contrast, general civil service exams assess a broad range of competencies applicable to multiple roles. These exams typically include questions on verbal and numerical reasoning, logical thinking, and general knowledge. General exams are used for entry-level positions where a broad skill set is advantageous, allowing candidates to qualify for various roles within the civil service.

Another important aspect to consider is the format of the exams. While many civil service exams are written, incorporating multiple-choice or essay questions, others may include practical components or oral interviews. Written exams primarily test a candidate's theoretical knowledge and cognitive abilities, while practical assessments evaluate hands-on skills and problem-solving capabilities in real-world scenarios. Oral interviews, often included in the selection process for managerial or senior roles, assess a candidate's communication skills, leadership potential, and ability to handle complex situations.

The scoring and evaluation criteria for civil service exams can also vary. Some exams use a pass/fail system, while others rank candidates based on their scores. In highly competitive positions, even a small difference in scores can significantly impact a candidate's ranking and chances of being selected. Understanding the scoring mechanism is crucial for candidates, as it influences study priorities and time management during the exam.

Importance of the Civil Service Exam

The civil service exam holds a pivotal role in shaping the future of public service. It is a cornerstone of democratic governance, ensuring that the individuals who fill public sector roles are selected based on merit, competence, and integrity. This exam is not merely a test of knowledge; it is a rigorous evaluation designed to identify candidates who possess the qualities and skills necessary to serve the public effectively.

At its core, the civil service exam is a tool for promoting fairness and equality in the hiring process. By standardizing the assessment of candidates, it eliminates biases that might otherwise influence hiring decisions. This meritocratic approach guarantees that positions in government are filled by qualified individuals, rather than through favoritism or nepotism. The importance of such a system cannot be overstated, as it upholds the principles of justice and transparency that are fundamental to public trust in government institutions.

One of the key reasons the civil service exam is crucial lies in its ability to maintain a high standard of public service. Government roles often involve complex decision-making, management of public resources, and implementation of policies that affect the entire community. The exam serves as a filter, ensuring that only those with the requisite knowledge, skills, and abilities are entrusted with these responsibilities. This is especially critical in areas such as public safety, healthcare, and education, where the impact of decisions can be profound and far-reaching.

The civil service exam also plays a significant role in fostering diversity within the public sector. By providing a level playing field, it encourages individuals from varied backgrounds to pursue careers in public service. This diversity is vital for a government that seeks to represent and serve a diverse population. The exam helps to break down barriers, allowing talented individuals from all walks of life to contribute to the governance and betterment of society.

Furthermore, the exam is a catalyst for personal and professional growth. Preparing for the civil service exam requires dedication, discipline, and a commitment to self-improvement. Candidates often engage in extensive study, honing their analytical skills, and gaining a deeper understanding of the functions and challenges of government. This process not only prepares them for the exam itself but also equips them with valuable skills and knowledge that will benefit them throughout their careers.

The civil service exam also serves as an indicator of a candidate's potential to adapt and thrive in a dynamic and evolving public service environment. The nature of government work is constantly changing, with new challenges and opportunities arising regularly. Candidates who succeed in the exam demonstrate not only their current competencies but also their ability to learn, grow, and adapt to future demands. This adaptability is a crucial trait for public servants, who must navigate the complexities of modern governance with agility and foresight.

Moreover, the civil service exam is instrumental in reinforcing the ethical standards expected of public servants. The exam process often includes assessments of a candidate's understanding of ethical principles, integrity, and accountability. These qualities are essential for maintaining public confidence in government institutions and for ensuring that public servants act in the best interests of the community. The exam helps to instill these values in candidates from the outset, setting the tone for their future conduct and decision-making.

The importance of the civil service exam extends beyond the individual to the broader society. Effective public service is the backbone of a functioning democracy, and the exam is a critical mechanism for ensuring that public institutions are staffed by individuals who are both capable and committed to serving the public good. This, in turn, contributes to the overall stability and prosperity of society, as well-functioning government institutions are better able to respond to the needs and aspirations of the community.

In addition, the civil service exam acts as a benchmark for continuous improvement within the public sector. By regularly updating and refining the exam content and format, governments can ensure that they are selecting candidates who are equipped to address contemporary challenges. This ongoing process of evaluation and adaptation helps to keep the public service vibrant, innovative, and responsive to change.

For individuals aspiring to enter the civil service, the exam represents a significant milestone on their career path. It is a gateway to opportunities for meaningful work, professional development, and the chance to make a tangible difference in the lives of others. The sense of purpose and fulfillment that comes from serving the public is a powerful motivator for many candidates, and the civil service exam is the first step towards realizing that potential.

Common Myths and Misconceptions

The journey towards a career in civil service is often clouded by a series of myths and misconceptions, which can deter potential candidates from pursuing this rewarding path. These misconceptions not only create unnecessary anxiety but also foster a misunderstanding of what the civil service exam truly entails. Dispelling these myths is essential for candidates to approach the exam with confidence and clarity.

One prevalent myth is the notion that the civil service exam is impossibly difficult, designed to filter out all but the most exceptional candidates. While it is true that the exam is challenging, it is by no means insurmountable. The purpose of the exam is to assess the skills and knowledge relevant to public service roles, not to create an impenetrable barrier. With diligent preparation, a clear understanding of the exam content, and a strategic study plan, candidates can certainly succeed.

Another common misconception is that the exam requires a level of intellectual prowess akin to that of a genius. This myth often discourages individuals who doubt their own abilities. In reality, the exam is structured to evaluate a candidate's aptitude for problem-solving, critical thinking, and understanding of basic principles related to the role they are applying for. It is not an IQ test nor a measure of innate intelligence. Rather, it is an assessment of learned skills and the ability to apply them effectively.

Many candidates also believe that only recent graduates or those with specific academic backgrounds are capable of passing the civil service exam. This myth perpetuates the idea that older individuals or those from diverse educational backgrounds are at a disadvantage. In fact, the civil service values diverse experiences and perspectives, recognizing that a varied workforce enriches public service. Successful candidates come from all walks of life, bringing with them unique insights and skills that benefit government operations.

A significant misconception concerns the role of luck in passing the exam. Some candidates attribute success to chance, believing that guessing answers can lead to a passing score. While there is an element of uncertainty in any multiple-choice test, relying on luck is not a viable strategy. The exam is designed to assess a deep understanding of the material, and educated guessing should only be used as a last resort. Thorough preparation remains the most reliable method for achieving a successful outcome.

There is also a myth that extensive rote memorization is the key to passing the civil service exam. While memorization of certain facts and figures can be helpful, the exam often focuses more on the application of knowledge rather than mere recall. Candidates are typically required to analyze scenarios, solve problems, and make informed decisions based on the information provided. Developing a comprehensive understanding of the material and practicing application through mock exams and situational questions is far more effective than rote memorization alone.

Another widespread misconception is that once you pass the civil service exam, a job is guaranteed. Many believe that success in the exam equates to automatic employment, which can lead to disappointment if they do not receive an immediate job offer. Passing the exam is certainly a significant achievement, but it is only one step in the hiring process. Candidates must also undergo interviews, background checks, and other evaluations before being offered a position. Understanding this process helps manage expectations and prepares candidates for the journey ahead.

Some individuals are under the false impression that connections or personal influence can bypass the need for taking the exam. This myth undermines the integrity of the civil service system, which is based on merit and equal opportunity. While networking and professional relationships can be beneficial in understanding the landscape of public service, they do not replace the requirement to succeed in the civil service exam. The exam remains a fundamental part of ensuring that all candidates are evaluated fairly and equitably.

A further misconception is that only those who have previously worked in government or public service are likely to pass the exam. Some candidates fear that their lack of direct experience in the sector will hinder their chances. However, the exam is designed to level the playing field, allowing individuals from various professional backgrounds to demonstrate their potential. The skills assessed by the exam—such as critical thinking, problem-solving, and communication—are not exclusive to public service and can be developed in a range of settings.

Many candidates also labor under the belief that the exam content is obscure or irrelevant to the actual job functions they will perform. This myth can lead to disengagement and a lack of motivation to study. In reality, the civil service exam is carefully constructed to reflect the competencies required for public service roles. The questions are designed to simulate real-world challenges and scenarios that candidates may encounter in their positions. Understanding the relevance of the exam content can enhance a candidate's engagement and commitment to their preparation.

Overview of the Book's Approach

Crafting a successful strategy for tackling the civil service exam requires a nuanced understanding of both the content and the methodology behind preparation. This book aims to equip aspirants with the knowledge and techniques necessary to navigate the process with confidence. Our approach is comprehensive yet practical, designed to demystify the exam and provide actionable insights that can be tailored to each individual's needs.

The journey begins with a clear-eyed view of what the civil service exam entails, moving beyond mere surface-level understanding. By delving into the intricacies of the exam format, candidates can better appreciate the rationale behind each section and question type. This foundational knowledge serves as a springboard, allowing candidates to structure their study plans in a way that maximizes efficiency and effectiveness.

One of the core tenets of the book's approach is the integration of theory and practice. While understanding the theoretical concepts behind the exam content is crucial, it is equally important to apply this knowledge through practical exercises. The book provides a variety of practice questions and scenarios, mirroring the kinds of challenges candidates will face in the actual exam. By engaging with these exercises, candidates develop the ability to think critically and apply their knowledge in context, which is essential for success.

Equally important is the emphasis on tailored study techniques that cater to diverse learning styles. Recognizing that each candidate approaches the exam from a unique perspective, the book offers a range of strategies to accommodate different preferences. Whether a candidate thrives on visual aids, auditory learning, or hands-on practice, the book outlines methods to enhance retention and understanding. This flexibility ensures that candidates can adapt their study plans to suit their individual strengths, ultimately fostering a more personalized and effective preparation experience.

The book also addresses the psychological aspects of exam preparation, acknowledging the role of mindset and mental resilience in achieving success. It provides insights into managing stress, building confidence, and maintaining focus throughout the preparation process. By fostering a positive and proactive mindset, candidates can approach the exam with a sense of empowerment and readiness.

In addition to technical knowledge and mental preparation, the book underscores the importance of strategic planning. Candidates are guided through the process of setting realistic goals, prioritizing study topics, and managing their time effectively. This strategic approach ensures that candidates allocate their resources wisely, concentrating their efforts on areas that will yield the greatest results.

Moreover, the book sheds light on the common pitfalls and mistakes that candidates often encounter during their preparation. By identifying these challenges, candidates can take proactive measures to avoid them, thereby streamlining their path to success. This proactive approach not only saves time but also enhances the overall quality of preparation.

Throughout the book, real-life examples and anecdotes from successful candidates are interwoven to provide context and inspiration. These stories serve as a reminder that the civil service exam is not an insurmountable obstacle, but a stepping stone towards a rewarding career in public service. By learning from the experiences of others, candidates can gain valuable insights and motivation to persevere in their own journeys.

The book's approach is also rooted in the principle of continuous improvement. Recognizing that preparation is an evolving process, candidates are encouraged to regularly assess their progress, identify areas for improvement, and adjust their strategies accordingly. This iterative process ensures that candidates remain adaptable and responsive to their own needs, ultimately leading to a more refined and successful preparation.

CHAPTER 2

MASTERING THE BASICS

Arithmetic and Number Operations

Arithmetic and number operations form the cornerstone of mathematical knowledge and are essential components of the civil service exam. A solid grasp of these fundamentals not only aids in tackling exam questions with confidence but also enhances problem-solving skills applicable to various real-world scenarios. Understanding the nuances of arithmetic is critical for anyone preparing to navigate the complexities of the civil service exam.

At the heart of arithmetic lies the four basic operations: addition, subtraction, multiplication, and division. Mastery of these operations is foundational, as they underpin more complex mathematical concepts tested in the civil service exam. Addition and subtraction are often the first operations candidates encounter, and they provide the basis for understanding the relationships between numbers. When approaching addition, it is important to recognize patterns and shortcuts, such as grouping numbers to make calculations faster and more efficient. Subtraction can be seen as the inverse of addition, and understanding this relationship helps in visualizing problems and checking work for accuracy.

Multiplication and division build on the principles of addition and subtraction but require a higher level of abstraction. Multiplication is essentially repeated addition, and recognizing this can simplify complex problems. For example, multiplying 7 by 5 can be approached as adding 7 five times. Division, on the other hand, is the process of distributing a number into equal parts. Understanding how multiplication and division are inverse operations allows candidates to verify results and approach problems from multiple angles.

Beyond the basic operations, the civil service exam often tests candidates on their ability to work with fractions, decimals, and percentages. These concepts are essential for interpreting data and solving practical problems. Fractions represent parts of a whole and require an understanding of numerators and denominators. Simplifying fractions, finding common denominators, and converting between improper fractions and mixed numbers are skills that candidates must hone. Practice with real-world examples, such as dividing a pizza among friends or calculating discounts, can make these concepts more relatable and easier to grasp.

Decimals are another critical aspect of arithmetic, and candidates must be comfortable with converting between decimals and fractions. Understanding place value is key to performing operations with decimals, whether adding, subtracting, multiplying, or dividing. To illustrate, when multiplying decimals, candidates should be mindful of the placement of the decimal point in the product. Likewise, when dividing, adjusting the decimal point appropriately in both the dividend and the divisor ensures accuracy.

Percentages play a vital role in interpreting data and understanding proportions. Mastery of percentages involves converting between percentages, fractions, and decimals, as well as calculating percentage increases, decreases, and changes. Real-life applications, such as calculating interest rates or analyzing statistical data, demonstrate the importance of percentages in everyday decision-making and problem-solving.

An often-overlooked aspect of arithmetic and number operations is estimation. Estimation is a powerful tool that allows candidates to check the reasonableness of their answers. By rounding numbers and making educated guesses, candidates can quickly approximate results, saving time and reducing the likelihood of errors. Estimation is particularly useful in scenarios where exact numbers are unnecessary or when assessing whether a calculated answer is within a plausible range.

Problem-solving strategies are integral to mastering arithmetic and number operations. Breaking complex problems into smaller, manageable parts can make them more approachable. Identifying patterns, relationships, and sequences among numbers can also simplify calculations. Additionally, visual aids, such as number lines or diagrams, can provide clarity and aid in understanding abstract concepts. Practicing these strategies regularly helps to build confidence and efficiency.

Time management is another crucial element of success in mastering arithmetic for the civil service exam. Allocating time wisely during the exam ensures that candidates can tackle all questions without feeling rushed. Practicing under timed conditions familiarizes candidates with the pace required to complete the exam and highlights areas where additional practice may be needed.

Developing a systematic approach to studying arithmetic is beneficial for long-term retention and understanding. Regular practice, combined with revisiting challenging concepts, reinforces knowledge and builds proficiency. Engaging with a variety of resources, such as textbooks, online tutorials, and practice exams, provides diverse perspectives and explanations, catering to different learning preferences.

Collaborative learning can also enhance arithmetic skills. Working with peers or study groups allows candidates to share strategies, clarify doubts, and gain new insights into problem-solving techniques. Discussions and group exercises foster a deeper understanding and provide opportunities to articulate mathematical concepts, reinforcing learning.

Maintaining a positive attitude and growth mindset is essential throughout the preparation process. Embracing challenges as opportunities for growth and viewing mistakes as valuable learning experiences empowers candidates to persist and improve. Confidence in arithmetic abilities grows with practice, and celebrating small victories along the way can boost motivation and commitment.

Basic Algebra and Problem Solving

Basic algebra serves as a crucial stepping stone in the realm of mathematics, especially when preparing for the civil service exam. It equips candidates with the tools needed to solve problems efficiently and think logically. Understanding algebraic concepts is not only essential for the exam but also invaluable in many aspects of decision-making and strategic planning in public service roles.

At the core of algebra are variables—symbols that represent unknown values or quantities. These variables allow us to formulate equations that can model real-world situations. Grasping the concept of variables is fundamental, as it leads to solving equations and inequalities, tasks frequently encountered in the civil service exam. For example, in a simple equation like $x+5=10x+5=10$, identifying the value of xx involves basic algebraic manipulation: subtracting 5 from both sides to isolate the variable, revealing $x=5x=5$.

Equations are also used to express relationships between quantities. Linear equations, which form straight lines when graphed, are among the simplest and most common types. They follow the standard form $y=mx+by=mx+b$, where mm represents the slope and bb the y-intercept. Understanding how to manipulate and solve linear equations is vital for answering questions that require analyzing trends or making predictions based on given data.

One practical application of linear equations is in budgeting and financial planning. Consider a scenario where a government department must allocate funding across various projects while adhering to a fixed budget. By representing each project's cost as a variable within an equation, planners can determine the most efficient distribution of resources to meet organizational goals.

Quadratic equations, another key algebraic concept, are slightly more complex, involving terms squared (e.g., $ax2+bx+c=0ax2+bx+c=0$). These equations can model various phenomena, such as projectile motion or optimization problems where finding maximum or minimum values is crucial. Solving quadratics typically involves factoring, completing the square, or applying the quadratic formula, each method offering a different approach to uncovering solutions.

Algebra also introduces inequalities, which express the relative size of two values rather than their equality. In real-world contexts, inequalities might represent budget constraints or population thresholds that must be met or exceeded. Solving inequalities involves similar steps to solving equations but requires careful attention to the direction of the inequality sign, especially when multiplying or dividing by negative numbers.

For civil service candidates, mastering these algebraic techniques enhances problem-solving abilities, enabling them to tackle a wide range of questions. Consider a situation where a candidate needs to optimize the allocation of resources to maximize efficiency without exceeding constraints. Algebraic inequalities can help identify feasible solutions within given limits, facilitating informed decision-making.

Problem-solving in algebra often involves translating word problems into mathematical expressions or equations. This skill is critical, as it bridges the gap between theoretical knowledge and practical application. To develop this ability, candidates should practice dissecting complex scenarios, identifying relevant information, and representing it algebraically. This process often begins with defining variables, creating equations based on relationships, and systematically solving for unknowns.

Developing a systematic approach to problem-solving is crucial. Candidates can begin by reading a problem carefully, identifying what is being asked, and determining the known and unknown quantities. Next, they should formulate an equation or inequality that represents the problem, taking care to align mathematical expressions with the scenario's context. Solving the equation and interpreting the result completes the process, providing a clear, logical solution to the problem at hand.

Additionally, practice is key to mastering algebra and enhancing problem-solving skills. Regularly engaging with a variety of algebraic problems helps solidify concepts and improve fluency. Candidates should explore different problem types, from simple linear equations to more complex quadratic or system-of-equations problems, to build confidence and versatility in their approach.

Using real-life applications of algebra can make learning more engaging and relevant. For instance, candidates might explore how algebra is used in calculating loan interest rates, analyzing population growth trends, or determining optimal production levels in an industrial context. By applying algebraic concepts to tangible scenarios, candidates can better appreciate the value and utility of their skills.

An often-underestimated aspect of problem-solving is the importance of verifying solutions. After solving an equation or inequality, candidates should substitute their solution back into the original expression to confirm its validity. This practice not only ensures accuracy but also reinforces understanding by demonstrating how the solution fits within the problem's framework.

Understanding Percentages and Ratios

Understanding percentages and ratios is crucial for anyone preparing for the civil service exam. These mathematical concepts are not just integral to the exam; they are also pivotal in analyzing data, making decisions, and solving problems in various public service roles. A firm grasp of percentages and ratios enhances one's ability to interpret information accurately and utilize it effectively in diverse scenarios.

Percentages are a way of expressing numbers as parts of a whole, specifically out of 100. This concept is widely used to describe proportions, changes, and comparisons in everyday life. For instance, when evaluating the effectiveness of a new policy or program, government officials often look at percentage increases or decreases in relevant metrics. Understanding percentages allows candidates to make sense of such data, facilitating informed decision-making.

One fundamental skill is converting between percentages, fractions, and decimals. This conversion is essential because percentages often appear alongside other numerical forms. For example, a budget might be presented in terms of percentages, but calculations may require the use of fractions or decimals. Mastery of these conversions enables candidates to switch seamlessly between different formats, ensuring they can handle any mathematical challenges they encounter.

Calculating percentage changes is another vital skill. This involves determining how much a quantity has increased or decreased relative to its original value. For example, if a city's population grows from 50,000 to 55,000, the percentage increase can be calculated by dividing the change (5,000) by the original amount (50,000) and then multiplying by 100, resulting in a 10% increase. Such calculations are common in civil service roles that involve monitoring trends and assessing policy impacts.

Percentages are also used to calculate proportions in scenarios such as allocating resources or analyzing demographic data. Consider a public health campaign targeting a specific percentage of a population; understanding how to translate that percentage into actual numbers is crucial for planning and implementation. Candidates should practice applying percentages to various contexts to build flexibility and confidence in their problem-solving abilities.

Ratios, on the other hand, express the relative size of two or more values. They provide a way to compare quantities and understand their relationships. A ratio might describe the number of teachers to students in a classroom or the distribution of funding across departments. Ratios are often presented in the form "a to b" or as a fraction, and understanding how to manipulate these expressions is essential for interpreting data accurately.

One key aspect of working with ratios is simplifying them to their lowest terms. This process involves dividing both terms of the ratio by their greatest common divisor. Simplifying ratios makes them easier to understand and compare, providing clarity when analyzing relationships between quantities. For example, a ratio of 50 to 100 can be simplified to 1 to 2, indicating that for every one unit of the first quantity, there are two units of the second.

Ratios are also used in proportion problems, where the goal is to determine how one quantity changes in relation to another. Solving proportions involves setting up an equation that equates two ratios and solving for the unknown. For instance, if a recipe requires 3 cups of flour for every 2 cups of sugar, and you have 9 cups of flour, you can use a proportion to find how much sugar is needed: $\frac{3}{2}=\frac{9}{x}$ $\frac{2}{3}=\frac{x}{9}$. Solving this equation reveals that 6 cups of sugar are required.

The concept of equivalent ratios is crucial, as it underpins the idea of scaling up or down while maintaining the same relationship between quantities. This concept is particularly relevant in fields such as urban planning, where scaling population density or infrastructure development requires accurate calculations to maintain proportional relationships.

Understanding the interplay between percentages and ratios is essential for interpreting complex data sets. For example, in analyzing a budget, percentages might reveal the proportion of total spending allocated to different departments, while ratios help compare spending between departments. Being able to switch between these perspectives allows candidates to gain a comprehensive understanding of financial data.

Real-world applications of percentages and ratios extend beyond mathematical calculations. They play a significant role in communication and decision-making processes. Public officials often use percentages to convey information about policy outcomes or program effectiveness to stakeholders. Being able to interpret and explain these figures clearly and accurately is crucial for maintaining transparency and accountability.

To master these concepts, candidates should engage in regular practice, using a variety of exercises and real-life scenarios. Practice not only reinforces understanding but also helps candidates develop the speed and accuracy needed for the civil service exam. Working with diverse problem types, from simple percentage calculations to complex ratio analyses, builds confidence and adaptability.

Visualization tools, such as pie charts or bar graphs, can aid in understanding percentages and ratios by providing a visual representation of data. These tools help candidates see relationships and proportions at a glance, enhancing their ability to interpret and communicate information effectively.

Estimation is another valuable skill when working with percentages and ratios. Being able to approximate values quickly can save time and provide a check on more detailed calculations. Estimation is particularly useful in scenarios where precise numbers are unnecessary or when verifying the plausibility of results.

Incorporating percentages and ratios into everyday decision-making and problem-solving activities helps candidates internalize these concepts. Whether analyzing personal finances, interpreting news reports, or planning a project, applying percentages and ratios in real-life contexts reinforces their relevance and utility.

Essential Grammar and Vocabulary

A strong command of grammar and vocabulary is indispensable for success in the civil service exam. These linguistic tools form the backbone of effective communication, enabling candidates to convey ideas clearly and persuasively. Mastering essential grammar and vocabulary not only enhances written and spoken communication skills but also aids in comprehending complex texts, a crucial aspect of the exam.

Grammar serves as the structural framework that governs the use of language. Understanding grammatical rules ensures that sentences are constructed logically and coherently. One fundamental aspect of grammar is sentence structure, which dictates the arrangement of words to form meaningful statements. A well-structured sentence typically includes a subject, verb, and object, providing clarity and precision. For instance, in the sentence "The committee approved the proposal," the subject (committee), verb (approved), and object (proposal) are clearly defined, leaving no ambiguity about the action taken.

Verb tense is another critical component of grammar, indicating the timing of actions or events. The civil service exam often requires candidates to discern the appropriate tense in various contexts, ensuring that narratives or reports are temporally accurate. Whether describing past initiatives, current policies, or future plans, selecting the correct tense is vital for conveying information accurately. For example, using the past tense in "The department implemented new measures last year" provides a clear temporal context, distinguishing past actions from ongoing or future ones.

Subject-verb agreement is an essential rule ensuring that subjects and verbs align in number, a common area of error in both writing and speech. Singular subjects require singular verbs, while plural subjects take plural verbs. Understanding this rule helps prevent mistakes that can obscure meaning and reduce credibility. Consider the sentence "The results of the study were conclusive," where the plural subject (results) correctly pairs with the plural verb (were).

Pronouns and their antecedents must also agree in number and gender, maintaining coherence throughout a text. Misalignment can lead to confusion, as in the sentence "Each participant provided their feedback," where the singular antecedent (participant) does not match the plural pronoun (their). Correcting this to "Each participant provided his or her feedback" ensures grammatical consistency.

Modifiers add detail and nuance to sentences, but misplaced modifiers can lead to unintended interpretations. Ensuring that modifiers are placed close to the words they describe is crucial for clarity. In the sentence "She almost drove her children to school every day," the placement of "almost" suggests she rarely drove her children, whereas "She drove her children to school almost every day" correctly conveys frequent action.

Punctuation marks, though small, wield significant power in shaping meaning. Commas, periods, semicolons, and colons each serve distinct functions, guiding readers through complex ideas. For example, a comma in "Let's eat, Grandma!" separates the speaker from the action, preventing a potentially humorous yet macabre misinterpretation as opposed to "Let's eat Grandma!" where the lack of comma changes the meaning drastically.

Transition words and phrases facilitate the flow of ideas, linking sentences and paragraphs seamlessly. Words like "however," "moreover," and "therefore" signal shifts in thought or introduce new information, aiding readers in following the writer's logic. Effective use of transitions enhances coherence, ensuring that arguments are presented logically and persuasively.

Building a rich vocabulary complements grammatical skills, allowing candidates to express themselves with precision and nuance. A diverse vocabulary empowers candidates to articulate complex ideas succinctly, avoiding ambiguity and repetition. For instance, replacing "very good" with "excellent" or "improve" with "enhance" elevates the quality of communication.

Contextual understanding is key to vocabulary acquisition. Learning words in context, rather than in isolation, aids retention and facilitates proper usage. Reading widely exposes candidates to diverse vocabulary and usage patterns, reinforcing understanding and expanding linguistic repertoire. Engaging with a variety of texts, from official reports to literary works, provides insight into formal and informal language styles.

Synonyms and antonyms enrich vocabulary by offering alternatives and contrasts. Familiarity with these relationships enables candidates to choose words that best fit the context, enhancing clarity and impact. For example, understanding that "diligent" is a synonym for "hardworking" and an antonym for "indolent" allows candidates to convey varying degrees of effort and work ethic.

Idiomatic expressions, though challenging, add color and depth to language. Understanding idioms enhances comprehension and communication, especially in contexts where literal interpretations fall short. For example, the phrase "break the ice" conveys initiating conversation rather than physically breaking ice, illustrating the importance of cultural and contextual awareness in language use.

Precision in language is vital for conveying accurate information and avoiding misunderstandings. Selecting words with specific meanings, rather than relying on vague or general terms, ensures that communication is clear and effective. For instance, describing a policy as "comprehensive" rather than simply "good" provides a clearer picture of its scope and impact.

Reading Comprehension Techniques

Reading comprehension is a fundamental skill essential for success in the civil service exam, and it extends far beyond simply understanding words on a page. It involves the ability to extract meaning, analyze content, and synthesize information effectively. Mastering reading comprehension techniques enhances one's ability to navigate the exam's diverse range of texts, from dense policy documents to brief news excerpts, and apply this understanding in real-world public service scenarios.

The cornerstone of reading comprehension is active reading, a technique that involves engaging with the text purposefully. Active reading requires a reader to interact with the material by asking questions, making predictions, and drawing connections. Before diving into a passage, it's beneficial to preview the text by skimming headings, subheadings, and any highlighted terms. This initial overview provides a framework that guides understanding and highlights key themes and concepts to look out for.

While reading, annotating can be a powerful tool. By underlining or highlighting important points, circling unfamiliar terms, and jotting down quick notes in the margins, readers create a personalized map of the text. This process aids in retention and allows for quick reference when reviewing or answering related questions. Annotations also serve as a visual cue of the text's structure, helping identify main ideas, supporting details, and points of contention.

Summarizing is another effective technique for enhancing comprehension. After reading a section, try to distill the information into a concise summary, capturing the main idea and key points. This practice not only reinforces understanding but also improves memory retention. In preparation for the civil service exam, developing the ability to summarize effectively is invaluable, as it enables candidates to quickly convey essential information in both written and verbal formats.

Inferencing, or reading between the lines, is a more advanced comprehension skill that involves drawing conclusions based on implicit information. Authors often imply rather than state information directly, requiring readers to piece together clues from the text. Practice inferencing by considering what the author implies but does not explicitly say, and examine how context and tone influence interpretation. Developing this skill enhances critical thinking and aids in understanding nuanced or complex materials.

Contextual understanding is crucial for interpreting unfamiliar vocabulary and dense passages. Rather than relying solely on dictionary definitions, readers can use surrounding words and sentences to infer meaning. This skill is particularly useful when encountering technical jargon or specialized terminology that might appear in policy documents or reports. Understanding context helps bridge gaps in knowledge and ensures a more holistic grasp of the material.

Recognizing text structure is another important aspect of reading comprehension. Different texts follow various organizational patterns, such as cause and effect, compare and contrast, or problem and solution. Identifying these structures enables readers to anticipate the flow of information and locate specific details more efficiently. For instance, a problem-solution text will typically present an issue followed by proposed resolutions, guiding the reader through a logical progression.

Critical analysis involves evaluating an author's arguments, evidence, and conclusions. Distinguishing between fact and opinion, assessing the credibility of sources, and identifying biases are key components of this skill. By questioning the reliability and validity of the information presented, readers develop a more discerning eye, crucial for interpreting policy documents, reports, or persuasive essays. This analytical approach ensures that candidates can make informed judgments based on sound reasoning and evidence.

Practicing reading comprehension across diverse genres and formats is essential for building adaptability and versatility. Exposure to a wide range of materials, such as news articles, research papers, and opinion pieces, familiarizes candidates with different writing styles, tones, and complexity levels. This variety prepares them to confidently tackle any text the civil service exam might present, from straightforward instructions to intricate policy analyses.

Time management is a critical component of effective reading comprehension, especially in an exam setting where time is limited. Developing the ability to read efficiently without sacrificing understanding is key. Practicing under timed conditions helps candidates gauge their reading speed and identify areas where they might need to increase efficiency. Techniques like skimming for main ideas or scanning for specific details can save valuable time while ensuring comprehensive coverage of the material.

Engaging in discussions or study groups can further enhance reading comprehension skills. Sharing interpretations, debating viewpoints, and exploring different perspectives fosters a deeper understanding of texts. This collaborative approach encourages active engagement and allows candidates to refine their analytical and critical thinking skills through dialogue and feedback.

CHAPTER 3

ADVANCED VERBAL SKILLS

Synonyms, Antonyms, and Analogies

Building advanced verbal skills is crucial for anyone aspiring to excel in the civil service exam. Among the essential components of these skills are the understanding and application of synonyms, antonyms, and analogies. These elements not only enhance vocabulary but also improve the ability to interpret and articulate complex ideas. Mastery of these verbal tools enables candidates to navigate the exam's language sections with precision and confidence, as well as communicate effectively in their future roles.

Synonyms are words with similar meanings. Recognizing and utilizing synonyms enriches language by providing multiple ways to express a concept, which is invaluable in both written and spoken communication. For instance, the word "important" can be substituted with "crucial," "vital," or "significant," each carrying a slightly different nuance but conveying the same core idea. This flexibility allows candidates to tailor their language to suit the tone and context of a given situation, whether drafting a formal report or engaging in a casual conversation.

To effectively use synonyms, it's important to understand the subtle differences in connotation and context. Words that appear synonymous in a dictionary might carry distinct implications in practice. For example, "frugal" and "stingy" both relate to saving money, yet "frugal" often implies prudence, while "stingy" suggests an unwillingness to spend. Awareness of these nuances ensures that language remains precise and appropriate, avoiding potential misunderstandings.

Antonyms, words with opposite meanings, are equally significant in developing verbal dexterity. They provide a means to draw contrasts and highlight differences, which is particularly useful in analytical writing and persuasive arguments. For instance, contrasting "optimistic" with "pessimistic" can clarify a discussion about attitudes toward future outcomes. Understanding antonyms broadens vocabulary and enhances the ability to articulate complex ideas by emphasizing distinctions.

Incorporating antonyms into language requires careful consideration of context, just as with synonyms. Words that function as antonyms in one scenario might not apply universally. For example, "light" and "heavy" are antonyms when discussing weight, but in terms of color or mood, their opposites might differ. Developing an intuitive sense of when and how to employ antonyms enriches communication and ensures clarity.

Analogies, comparisons between two things based on similarity, are powerful tools for illustrating relationships and explaining abstract concepts. They are commonly used in the civil service exam to assess logical reasoning and critical thinking. Analogies require identifying a relationship between a pair of words and applying that relationship to another pair. For instance, "finger is to hand as toe is to foot" illustrates a part-to-whole relationship that aids in understanding complex systems or structures.

Creating effective analogies involves recognizing patterns and parallels across different contexts. This skill enhances one's ability to draw connections between disparate ideas, a valuable asset in problem-solving and innovation. By mastering analogies, candidates can convey intricate concepts in a relatable manner, facilitating comprehension and engagement with their audience.

Practicing with synonyms, antonyms, and analogies prepares candidates for the verbal challenges of the civil service exam. Regular exposure to varied texts, such as literature, essays, and technical documents, expands vocabulary and deepens understanding of word relationships. Additionally, engaging in exercises that require identifying and generating synonyms, antonyms, and analogies reinforces these skills and builds confidence.

Contextual learning plays a crucial role in mastering advanced verbal skills. Encountering words and expressions in context, rather than in isolation, aids retention and comprehension. Reading widely exposes candidates to diverse linguistic styles and usage patterns, which enhances their ability to apply verbal skills flexibly and adaptively.

Developing an awareness of linguistic subtleties, such as tone, register, and cultural nuances, is essential for effective communication. The same word might convey different meanings or levels of formality depending on the context. For example, "inform" is neutral, while "notify" can be more formal, and "tell" is casual. Understanding these distinctions ensures that language remains appropriate and effective across various settings.

Critical Reading Strategies

In the realm of advanced verbal skills, critical reading stands out as one of the most crucial abilities to develop, especially for those preparing for the civil service exam. Critical reading goes beyond mere comprehension of text; it involves engaging with the material on a deeper level, analyzing its structure, assessing its arguments, and evaluating its relevance and credibility. This skill is invaluable not only in exam settings but also in the professional world, where the ability to understand and critique complex documents is paramount.

One of the foundational aspects of critical reading is identifying the author's purpose and perspective. Every piece of writing is crafted with an intent, whether to inform, persuade, entertain, or a combination of these. Understanding this purpose helps readers discern the angle from which the author approaches a topic. For instance, a policy document aims to inform and direct, whereas an opinion editorial seeks to persuade. Recognizing the purpose provides context and clarifies the lens through which the content should be interpreted.

Assessing the credibility of a text is another vital component of critical reading. This involves examining the author's qualifications, the publication's reputation, and the sources cited within the document. Reliable texts typically present evidence-based arguments, cite reputable sources, and maintain objectivity. In contrast, texts with biased language, lack of evidence, or questionable sources warrant skepticism. Developing the ability to discern credible information ensures that candidates are equipped to make informed decisions based on trustworthy data.

Critical reading also requires analyzing the structure and organization of a text. Effective writing follows a logical progression, with clear introductions, coherent body paragraphs, and concise conclusions. Identifying this structure aids in understanding the flow of ideas and how they interconnect. For instance, a well-organized argumentative essay will present a thesis statement, followed by supporting evidence and counterarguments, leading to a reasoned conclusion. Recognizing these structural elements enhances comprehension and facilitates effective note-taking.

Evaluating arguments and evidence is central to critical reading. This involves scrutinizing the logic and reasoning behind an author's claims, identifying assumptions, and assessing the validity of the evidence presented. Readers should consider whether the arguments are supported by empirical data, whether the conclusions logically follow from the premises, and whether any logical fallacies are present. This analytical approach empowers candidates to engage with texts thoughtfully and form their own informed opinions.

Critical readers also pay attention to language and tone, which can reveal underlying biases or intentions. The choice of words, the use of rhetorical devices, and the overall tone contribute to the text's impact and meaning. For example, emotionally charged language might indicate an attempt to persuade through appeal rather than logic, while neutral language suggests an objective presentation of facts. Being attuned to these linguistic cues enables readers to better understand the author's intent and the potential influence on the audience.

Another important strategy is contextualizing the information. This involves situating the content within broader historical, cultural, or social frameworks. Understanding the context in which a text was written provides insight into its relevance and implications. For instance, a policy proposal might be better understood when considered alongside current socio-political events or historical precedents.

Contextualization enriches comprehension and allows readers to appreciate the text's significance within a larger narrative.

Practicing critical reading across a variety of genres and mediums enhances versatility and adaptability. Engaging with diverse materials, such as academic journals, news articles, speeches, and reports, exposes candidates to different writing styles, argumentation techniques, and complexity levels. This diversity prepares them for the wide range of texts they may encounter on the civil service exam and in their professional roles.

Time management is an essential aspect of critical reading, especially in exam scenarios where time is limited. Developing strategies to read efficiently without sacrificing depth of understanding is key. Techniques like skimming for main ideas, scanning for specific information, and prioritizing sections based on relevance can save time while ensuring a comprehensive grasp of the material. Practicing these techniques under timed conditions helps candidates build the speed and accuracy needed for success.

Effective Communication Skills

Effective communication is at the heart of success in both the civil service exam and the broader sphere of public service. It encompasses the ability to convey information clearly, engage in meaningful dialogue, and build relationships through language. Mastering these skills not only aids in exam performance but also paves the way for effective leadership and collaboration in professional settings.

Communication is a multifaceted skill that involves both verbal and non-verbal elements. Verbal communication includes the words we choose and how we structure them into sentences. Clarity and conciseness are paramount; they ensure that the audience understands the message without unnecessary complexity. In exam scenarios, where time and space are limited, candidates must articulate their thoughts succinctly, avoiding verbosity while maintaining the essence of their message.

Active listening is a crucial component of effective communication. It involves fully engaging with the speaker, understanding their message, and responding thoughtfully. This skill is essential in both personal interactions and professional settings, where listening to colleagues, stakeholders, or constituents can lead to more informed decision-making. Active listening requires attention, patience, and the ability to refrain from interrupting, allowing the speaker to fully express their thoughts.

Non-verbal communication, including body language, facial expressions, and tone of voice, significantly impacts how messages are received. These cues can reinforce or contradict spoken words, influencing the perception of sincerity, confidence, and enthusiasm. Understanding and effectively utilizing non-verbal signals enhance communication, ensuring that the intended message is conveyed accurately. For example, maintaining eye contact can demonstrate confidence and engagement, while an enthusiastic tone can energize and motivate an audience.

Storytelling is a powerful tool in communication, allowing speakers to engage their audience emotionally and intellectually. A well-crafted story can illustrate complex ideas, make abstract concepts relatable, and foster a connection between the speaker and the audience. When preparing for the civil service exam, candidates can use storytelling techniques to create compelling narratives in their essays or presentations, making their arguments more persuasive and memorable.

Empathy plays a significant role in effective communication, enabling individuals to connect with others by understanding their perspectives and emotions. Empathetic communication fosters trust and rapport, essential for collaborative problem-solving and conflict resolution. In public service, where understanding diverse viewpoints is crucial, empathy helps bridge gaps and build consensus, leading to more effective governance and service delivery.

Adaptability is another key aspect of communication. Different contexts, audiences, and purposes require different communication styles. For instance, a formal presentation to senior officials demands a different approach than a community meeting or a team discussion. Being able to adjust language, tone, and delivery to suit the audience and context enhances the effectiveness of communication, ensuring that the message resonates and achieves its intended impact.

Feedback is an integral part of the communication process, providing insights into how messages are received and understood. Constructive feedback helps individuals refine their communication skills, identify areas for improvement, and build confidence in their abilities. Seeking feedback from peers, mentors, or supervisors can illuminate blind spots and guide personal and professional development.

Conflict resolution skills are an essential component of effective communication, particularly in environments where differing opinions and interests are common. The ability to navigate disagreements, mediate disputes, and find common ground is invaluable in achieving successful outcomes. Effective conflict resolution involves active listening, empathy, negotiation, and the ability to remain calm and objective under pressure.

Writing Clarity and Conciseness

Writing with clarity and conciseness is an indispensable skill for anyone preparing for the civil service exam. The ability to articulate thoughts clearly and succinctly is crucial not only for exam success but also for effective communication in professional settings. These skills enable candidates to convey complex ideas efficiently, ensuring that their messages are understood without unnecessary embellishment or ambiguity.

At the heart of clear writing is the organization of ideas. When thoughts are structured logically, the reader can easily follow the progression of arguments or narratives. One effective method is to begin with a strong thesis statement or main idea, followed by supporting details and examples, and concluding with a summary or call to action. This structure guides the reader through the text, providing a roadmap that enhances comprehension.

Sentence structure plays a significant role in achieving clarity. Varied sentence lengths and structures maintain reader interest and help emphasize key points. Simple sentences convey straightforward information, while complex sentences can express more nuanced ideas. However, it's essential to avoid overly complex sentences that might confuse the reader. Each sentence should serve a purpose, advancing the argument or narrative without adding unnecessary complexity.

Word choice is another critical element of writing clarity. Precision in language ensures that the intended message is delivered accurately. This involves selecting words that convey the exact meaning without ambiguity. For example, instead of using a vague term like "thing," a more specific noun such as "device" or "procedure" provides clarity. Additionally, avoiding jargon or technical terms that the audience might not understand is crucial unless their use is necessary and adequately explained.

Conciseness in writing means eliminating superfluous words and phrases that do not add value to the content. Redundancies, filler words, and repetitive expressions can dilute the impact of writing. For instance, phrases like "at this point in time" can be simplified to "now," and "in order to" can be reduced to "to." By streamlining language, the writer ensures that each word contributes to the overall message, enhancing its effectiveness.

Active voice is preferable to passive voice for clarity and directness. Active voice places the subject at the forefront, making the sentence more dynamic and easier to understand. For example, "The committee approved the proposal" is clearer and more direct than "The proposal was approved by the committee." While passive voice may be appropriate in certain contexts, using active voice as a default enhances readability and engagement.

Transitions are vital for guiding the reader through the text and illustrating connections between ideas. Words and phrases like "however," "moreover," "as a result," and "in contrast" signal shifts in thought and help maintain the flow of the narrative or argument. Effective transitions prevent abrupt jumps between ideas, ensuring that the writing is cohesive and seamless.

Revising and editing are integral to achieving clarity and conciseness. The first draft is rarely perfect, and refining the text involves reviewing it with a critical eye. This process includes checking for grammatical errors, simplifying complex sentences, and trimming unnecessary content. Reading the text aloud can also help identify awkward phrasing or unclear passages, providing an opportunity to make adjustments before the final version.

Feedback from others can be invaluable during the editing process. Peers, mentors, or colleagues can offer fresh perspectives and identify areas for improvement that the writer might have overlooked. Constructive criticism helps refine writing skills and enhances the overall quality of the work.

Logical Reasoning and Deduction

Logical reasoning and deduction are foundational components of advanced verbal skills, particularly for those preparing for the civil service exam. These cognitive abilities allow individuals to analyze information, identify patterns, and draw informed conclusions. Mastering logical reasoning and deduction not only enhances problem-solving skills but also equips candidates to navigate complex scenarios in both academic and professional contexts.

At the core of logical reasoning is the ability to evaluate arguments critically. This involves assessing the validity and soundness of claims based on the evidence presented. A valid argument is one wherein the conclusion logically follows from the premises. Soundness, on the other hand, requires that the argument is both valid and based on true premises. For example, consider the argument: "All public servants are dedicated. Maria is a public servant. Therefore, Maria is dedicated." This argument is both valid and sound if the premises are indeed true.

Understanding logical fallacies is crucial in evaluating arguments. Fallacies are errors in reasoning that undermine the logic of an argument. Common fallacies include ad hominem attacks, where the focus is on the person rather than the argument; straw man arguments, which misrepresent an opponent's position; and false dilemmas, which present limited options when more exist. Recognizing these fallacies enables candidates to dissect arguments more effectively and avoid being swayed by flawed reasoning.

Deductive reasoning involves deriving specific conclusions from general principles or premises. It follows a top-down approach, where the conclusion is a logical outcome of the premises. For instance, if the general rule is "All humans are mortal," and the specific case is "Socrates is a human," then the conclusion "Socrates is mortal" naturally follows. Deductive reasoning is precise and reliable, provided the premises are true, making it a powerful tool in both academic and professional settings.

Inductive reasoning, contrastingly, involves drawing general conclusions from specific observations. It follows a bottom-up approach, where patterns or trends are identified from individual cases. While inductive reasoning is not as conclusive as deductive reasoning, it is invaluable in forming hypotheses, making predictions, and generating new ideas. For example, observing that the sun rises in the east every morning might lead to the general conclusion that the sun always rises in the east.

Developing strong logical reasoning and deduction skills requires practice and exposure to diverse problems and scenarios. Engaging in activities such as puzzles, brainteasers, and logic games stimulates cognitive processes and enhances analytical abilities. Additionally, reading widely across genres, including philosophy, science, and literature, provides opportunities to encounter and evaluate various forms of reasoning.

Critical thinking plays a pivotal role in logical reasoning and deduction. It involves questioning assumptions, evaluating evidence, and weighing alternatives. Critical thinkers approach problems with an open mind, considering multiple perspectives before arriving at a conclusion. This approach not only enriches understanding but also fosters creativity and innovation.

The ability to construct well-reasoned arguments is essential for effective communication. Whether writing an essay, delivering a presentation, or participating in a debate, the clarity and persuasiveness of an argument depend on its logical structure. Constructing arguments involves identifying the main claim, supporting it with evidence, and addressing counterarguments. This structured approach ensures that the argument is coherent, compelling, and resilient to criticism.

Logical reasoning and deduction are also integral to decision-making processes. In professional settings, individuals are often required to assess complex situations, weigh potential outcomes, and make informed decisions. By applying logical reasoning, candidates can evaluate the pros and cons of different options, anticipate potential consequences, and choose the most effective course of action.

CHAPTER 4

MATHEMATICAL PROFICIENCY

Advanced Word Problems

Advanced word problems present a unique challenge in the civil service exam, testing not only mathematical proficiency but also the ability to interpret and apply mathematical concepts in real-world scenarios. These problems require a blend of analytical thinking, problem-solving skills, and an understanding of mathematical principles. Excelling in this area equips candidates with the tools needed to tackle complex quantitative tasks that are often encountered in public service roles.

To begin with, understanding the problem is crucial. Word problems often contain a wealth of information, and the first step is to identify what is being asked. Carefully reading the problem helps isolate the key pieces of information and the mathematical operations needed to find the solution. At times, irrelevant details may be included to test the candidate's ability to discern essential data from the extraneous. Developing a habit of annotating or highlighting important figures and keywords can be immensely helpful.

Translating words into mathematical expressions is the next critical step. This involves converting the narrative of the problem into equations or formulas that can be solved mathematically. Common phrases like "the sum of," "more than," and "product of" should trigger recognition of specific operations such as addition, subtraction, and multiplication. Becoming familiar with these verbal cues reduces the cognitive load during exams, allowing for quicker and more accurate translation.

Visualization can be a powerful tool in solving advanced word problems. Drawing diagrams, charts, or tables can help organize the information and make complex relationships clearer. This visual representation often provides insights into the problem that may not be immediately obvious from the text alone. For example, problems involving distances, areas, or volumes can often be simplified by sketching the scenario, which helps in identifying the relationships between different elements.

Once the problem has been translated into a mathematical form, the next step is solving the equations. This might involve algebraic manipulations, applying formulas, or using logical reasoning to arrive at the solution. It's important to work systematically, checking each step to ensure accuracy and prevent errors. In many cases, word problems will involve multiple steps or interrelated calculations, so keeping track of each part of the process is essential.

Time management is a key factor in handling advanced word problems during the civil service exam. Practicing under timed conditions helps build the ability to work efficiently without sacrificing accuracy. Candidates should aim to allocate time based on the complexity of the problem, tackling simpler problems first to secure easy points before moving on to more challenging ones. This strategy not only maximizes scores but also boosts confidence as candidates progress through the exam.

A common pitfall in solving word problems is jumping to conclusions without thoroughly analyzing the problem. It's crucial to avoid assumptions that aren't supported by the information given. For instance, if a problem involves rates or proportions, ensure that all units are consistent before performing calculations. Misinterpretation of units or relationships can lead to incorrect answers, even if the mathematical manipulations are performed correctly.

Reviewing and double-checking work is a valuable step that should not be overlooked. After arriving at a solution, it's beneficial to revisit the problem to verify that the answer makes sense in the context of the question. This review process can catch mistakes that might have been overlooked in the initial solution, such as miscalculations or misinterpretations of the problem.

Advanced word problems often integrate multiple mathematical concepts, such as algebra, geometry, and statistics. Familiarity with these areas and their applications is crucial. Strengthening foundational skills in each of these domains allows candidates to tackle a broader range of problems with confidence. Regular practice with a variety of problem types enhances flexibility and adaptability, preparing candidates for the diverse challenges they may face in the exam.

Geometry and Spatial Reasoning

Geometry and spatial reasoning are integral components of mathematical proficiency, particularly in the context of the civil service exam. These skills involve understanding shapes, sizes, relative positions, and properties of space, which are essential for interpreting and solving real-world problems. Developing a strong foundation in geometry and spatial reasoning equips candidates with the tools necessary to excel in both the exam and their subsequent roles in public service.

At the heart of geometry lies the study of shapes and their properties. Familiarity with basic geometric shapes such as triangles, circles, squares, and polygons is crucial. Each shape has distinct properties, such as angles, sides, and symmetry, which can be leveraged to solve complex problems. For instance, understanding that the sum of the angles in a triangle always equals 180 degrees allows candidates to find unknown angles when other angles are known. Similarly, recognizing properties of parallel lines and transversals can help solve problems involving angles and distances.

Spatial reasoning, on the other hand, involves the ability to visualize and manipulate objects in space. This skill is particularly useful when dealing with three-dimensional shapes. Being able to mentally rotate, flip, or transform objects enhances a candidate's ability to understand and solve problems involving volume, surface area, and spatial relationships. For example, visualizing how a cube can be unfolded into a two-dimensional net aids in calculating its surface area.

One effective way to develop spatial reasoning skills is through hands-on practice with physical models or digital tools that allow manipulation of shapes. Engaging with puzzles, building blocks, or software that simulates three-dimensional environments can significantly enhance spatial awareness. This practice not only reinforces theoretical knowledge but also helps in visualizing complex scenarios during the exam.

Understanding geometric principles also involves mastering the use of formulas to calculate perimeter, area, and volume. Memorizing these formulas is just the beginning; applying them correctly requires a clear understanding of when and how to use each one. For instance, knowing that the area of a circle is calculated using the formula $A=\pi r^2$ is vital, but understanding the derivation of this formula deepens comprehension and aids in solving more challenging problems.

Coordinate geometry, which involves plotting points, lines, and shapes on a grid, is another key aspect of geometry that appears frequently in the civil service exam. This branch of geometry allows candidates to solve problems involving distance, midpoint, and slope using algebraic techniques. Being able to translate between graphical and algebraic representations of shapes is a valuable skill that enhances problem-solving efficiency.

In addition to mastering formulas, candidates should develop an intuitive sense of measurement and estimation. This involves making quick, reasonable approximations of distances, areas, and volumes without relying solely on calculations. Estimation skills are particularly useful in multiple-choice scenarios where precise calculations may be time-consuming, allowing candidates to eliminate implausible options and focus on likely solutions.

Geometry and spatial reasoning also play a crucial role in interpreting and solving word problems. Many real-world scenarios require candidates to apply geometric concepts to find solutions. For example, determining the optimum layout for a new park, calculating the amount of materials needed for construction, or analyzing traffic patterns all require a solid understanding of geometric principles. Practicing with diverse problem sets helps candidates develop the ability to apply their knowledge flexibly and creatively.

Moreover, geometry often intersects with other areas of mathematics, such as algebra and trigonometry. Understanding these connections enhances problem-solving capabilities and provides a more comprehensive mathematical foundation. For instance, the Pythagorean theorem, which relates the sides of a right triangle, is a fundamental geometric principle that also involves algebraic manipulation. Recognizing these intersections allows candidates to approach problems from multiple angles, increasing the likelihood of finding efficient solutions.

To build proficiency in geometry and spatial reasoning, candidates should engage in regular practice with a variety of problems, ranging from basic to advanced levels. This practice should include both solitary study and collaborative learning, as discussing problems with peers can reveal new strategies and insights. Additionally, seeking feedback from instructors or mentors can guide improvement and highlight areas that require further attention.

Data Interpretation and Analysis

Data interpretation and analysis are pivotal skills for candidates facing the civil service exam, where the ability to make sense of numerical and graphical information is frequently tested. These skills are not merely academic exercises but critical competencies required in public service roles where decision-making often relies on the interpretation of complex datasets.

One of the first steps in mastering data interpretation is understanding different types of data presentations. Tables, charts, and graphs are commonly used formats, each with its unique features and methods of conveying information. Tables provide detailed numerical data, often requiring careful examination to discern trends or patterns. Charts and graphs, including bar charts, line graphs, and pie charts, offer visual representations that can make it easier to compare data points or identify relationships at a glance.

To effectively interpret data, candidates must first familiarize themselves with these formats, understanding how to extract relevant information from each. For instance, when examining a bar chart, attention should be paid to the axes, which define the categories and values being compared. Line graphs can illustrate trends over time, while pie charts can show proportions within a whole. Recognizing the strengths and limitations of each format aids in selecting the most appropriate type for different data sets and questions.

Critical to data interpretation is the ability to draw meaningful conclusions from the information presented. This involves not only identifying patterns and trends but also understanding the context and implications of the data. For example, a line graph showing a steady increase in population over several decades might suggest a need for expanded public services or infrastructure development. However, without additional context—such as the geographic region, factors contributing to the growth, or comparisons with other areas—it's challenging to form a complete picture.

Another essential aspect is the analysis of statistical measures such as mean, median, mode, and range. These metrics provide insights into the data's central tendency and variability. Understanding how to calculate and interpret these measures is fundamental, as they often form the basis of more complex analyses. For instance, knowing the mean income level in a region can guide policy decisions on economic development, but understanding the distribution of income (through measures like the range or standard deviation) provides a fuller understanding of economic inequality.

Spotting anomalies or outliers in data sets is another important skill. Outliers can skew results and lead to misinterpretations, so identifying them is crucial for accurate analysis. Understanding whether an outlier is due to an error, a unique circumstance, or an indicator of a broader trend requires critical thinking and sometimes further investigation.

Context is key when analyzing data. Without understanding the background or the conditions under which data was collected, conclusions may be flawed. For example, a sudden spike in sales figures could indicate a successful marketing campaign, but it might also be a result of seasonal demand or a one-time event. Evaluating data within its context ensures that interpretations are grounded in reality, reducing the risk of drawing erroneous conclusions.

Data interpretation often involves making comparisons. Whether comparing current data with historical data or contrasting different data sets, the ability to identify similarities and differences is vital. This might involve calculating percentage changes or differences in absolute terms, identifying correlations, or assessing trends over time. Such comparisons provide deeper insights and can highlight areas that require attention or further investigation.

Mathematical Reasoning

Mathematical reasoning is a critical skill for candidates preparing for the civil service exam, where the ability to apply logic and analytical thinking to mathematical problems is essential. This skill goes beyond mere calculation; it involves understanding the underlying principles and concepts that govern mathematical operations, enabling candidates to solve problems efficiently and accurately.

At its core, mathematical reasoning involves the ability to comprehend and manipulate abstract concepts. This begins with a firm grasp of fundamental mathematical principles, such as number theory, algebra, geometry, and statistics. Understanding these foundational elements is crucial, as they form the basis for more complex problem-solving tasks encountered in the exam. For instance, a strong knowledge of algebra allows candidates to solve equations and inequalities, while an understanding of geometry aids in tackling problems related to shapes and spatial relationships.

Mathematical reasoning also requires the ability to identify patterns and relationships within data. Recognizing these patterns can simplify complex problems and lead to more efficient solutions. For example, understanding the properties of arithmetic sequences can help candidates quickly find the sum of a series of numbers without having to perform each addition individually. Similarly, recognizing geometric patterns can aid in solving problems related to area and volume.

Another important aspect of mathematical reasoning is the ability to think critically and logically. This involves evaluating information, identifying assumptions, and drawing conclusions based on evidence. Critical thinking skills enable candidates to approach problems methodically, breaking them down into manageable parts and analyzing each component before arriving at a solution. This process not only enhances accuracy but also increases efficiency, as candidates learn to focus on the most relevant aspects of a problem while disregarding extraneous information.

Problem-solving strategies play a significant role in mathematical reasoning. Developing a repertoire of strategies, such as working backward, using trial and error, or employing estimation, provides candidates with a toolkit to tackle a wide range of problems. Each strategy has its strengths and weaknesses, and the key is to select the most appropriate one for a given problem. For instance, working backward can be particularly effective for problems with a clear end goal, while estimation is useful for quickly assessing the plausibility of a solution.

Visualization is a powerful tool in mathematical reasoning. Creating visual representations of problems, such as diagrams, graphs, or charts, can clarify complex relationships and make abstract concepts more tangible. Visualizing a problem often reveals insights that are not immediately apparent from the text alone, providing a clearer path to a solution. For example, sketching a geometric problem can help candidates see the relationships between different shapes and angles, leading to a more intuitive understanding of the problem.

Mathematical reasoning also involves the application of logic and deductive reasoning. Logical reasoning allows candidates to make connections between different pieces of information and draw valid conclusions. Deductive reasoning, in particular, involves deriving specific conclusions from general principles. For example, if candidates know that all angles in a triangle sum to 180 degrees, they can use this principle to find a missing angle when the other two are known. This type of reasoning is essential for solving problems that require the application of established mathematical laws and theorems.

Practice is crucial for developing mathematical reasoning skills. Regular engagement with a variety of problems, from simple to complex, helps candidates build familiarity and confidence in applying their reasoning skills. Practice also provides opportunities to experiment with different strategies, refine problem-solving techniques, and learn from mistakes. By encountering a diverse range of problems, candidates become more adaptable and better prepared to handle the unexpected challenges that may arise during the exam.

In addition to individual practice, collaborative learning can enhance mathematical reasoning. Discussing problems with peers, sharing strategies, and exploring different approaches can lead to new insights and a deeper understanding of mathematical concepts. Collaborative learning fosters a supportive environment where candidates can learn from each other, gain new perspectives, and build confidence in their abilities.

Calculator and Non-Calculator Techniques

Calculator and non-calculator techniques are essential tools for candidates preparing for the civil service exam, where proficiency in both methods can significantly influence performance. While calculators offer speed and accuracy for complex calculations, mastering non-calculator techniques ensures that candidates are not solely reliant on technology and are able to tackle problems that require mental agility and manual computation.

Understanding when to use a calculator is the first step towards maximizing efficiency. Calculators are invaluable for handling intricate calculations that involve large numbers, decimals, or fractions. They can quickly perform operations that would be time-consuming and prone to error if done manually. However, it's important to be familiar with the functions of the calculator, including basic operations, memory functions, and any advanced features that might be permitted during the exam. A calculator is only as effective as its user, so regular practice with the device ensures that candidates can use it swiftly and accurately under exam conditions.

Despite the advantages of calculators, non-calculator techniques are equally important, particularly because some parts of the exam may restrict their use. These techniques require a strong understanding of mathematical concepts and the ability to perform calculations manually. Developing mental math skills is crucial, as it allows candidates to make quick estimations and perform basic arithmetic without the aid of technology. Mental math is not only useful for solving problems directly but also for checking the plausibility of calculator results.

Being able to perform basic arithmetic operations manually is foundational. Addition, subtraction, multiplication, and division are core skills that underpin more complex mathematical tasks. Techniques such as breaking down numbers into smaller components, using multiplication tables, and employing division shortcuts can speed up manual calculations. For example, understanding that multiplying by 5 can be done by multiplying by 10 and then halving the result can simplify mental calculations significantly.

Estimation is another key non-calculator technique. Estimation involves rounding numbers to simplify calculations and quickly assess the reasonableness of an answer. This skill is particularly useful in multiple-choice questions, where an approximate answer can help eliminate implausible options. Estimation also serves as a valuable check on calculator results, ensuring that any input errors are caught before they lead to incorrect answers.

The ability to simplify complex problems through the application of mathematical properties is a valuable non-calculator skill. Recognizing patterns and relationships within numbers allows candidates to apply properties such as the distributive, associative, and commutative laws to streamline calculations. For instance, understanding that $a\times(b+c)=(a\times b)+(a\times c)$ can simplify problems involving multiplication and addition.

Working with fractions, decimals, and percentages is another area where non-calculator techniques are essential. Converting between these forms, simplifying fractions, and calculating percentages require a solid grasp of mathematical principles and the ability to perform precise manual calculations. Techniques such as finding common denominators, using proportional reasoning, and understanding decimal place value are integral to solving these types of problems efficiently.

Algebraic manipulation is a non-calculator technique that plays a significant role in solving equations and inequalities. Being able to rearrange equations, factor expressions, and solve for unknowns without a calculator is a skill that requires practice and a deep understanding of algebraic rules. Candidates should focus on mastering techniques such as isolating variables, combining like terms, and using substitution effectively.

Speed and accuracy in non-calculator techniques come with practice. Regular engagement with a variety of problems helps candidates build confidence in their manual calculation abilities. Timed practice sessions can simulate exam conditions, teaching candidates to work efficiently under pressure. Additionally, reviewing mistakes and seeking feedback from instructors or peers can highlight areas for improvement and reinforce learning.

Balancing the use of calculator and non-calculator techniques is crucial for success on the civil service exam. While calculators offer convenience and precision, non-calculator skills ensure that candidates are flexible and adaptable, able to tackle problems from multiple angles. By developing proficiency in both methods, candidates prepare themselves for the diverse range of challenges they may encounter in the exam.

CHAPTER 5

OFFICE PRACTICES AND PROCEDURES

Understanding Clerical Tasks

Clerical tasks form the backbone of many roles within the civil service, ensuring that organizations run smoothly and efficiently. These tasks encompass a range of activities, from managing records and documents to providing administrative support and facilitating communication within and outside the organization. For candidates preparing for the civil service exam, understanding these tasks is crucial, as they often form a significant portion of the responsibilities in public service roles.

At the heart of clerical work is effective document management. This involves creating, organizing, maintaining, and retrieving documents and records in both physical and digital formats. A well-organized filing system is essential, as it allows for quick access to information when needed. Candidates should familiarize themselves with common filing systems, such as alphabetical, numerical, and subject-based systems, and understand the principles of each. Additionally, proficiency in using electronic document management systems (EDMS) is increasingly important, as many organizations transition to digital records.

Data entry is another fundamental clerical task. This requires accuracy, attention to detail, and speed, as even minor errors can lead to significant issues down the line. Candidates should practice entering data into spreadsheets, databases, and other software applications, ensuring they are comfortable with the tools and processes involved. Mastery of keyboard shortcuts and touch typing can enhance efficiency, allowing candidates to complete tasks more quickly without sacrificing accuracy.

Communication is a vital component of clerical work, involving both written and verbal interactions. Drafting correspondence, such as emails, letters, and reports, requires clarity, professionalism, and attention to detail. Candidates should develop strong writing skills, focusing on grammar, punctuation, and style to ensure their communications are clear and effective. Additionally, verbal communication skills are essential, as clerical roles often involve answering phones, greeting visitors, and interacting with colleagues and clients. Practicing active listening and clear articulation can improve these skills, ensuring that candidates are well-prepared for the demands of the role.

Scheduling and time management are also key aspects of clerical tasks. This includes managing calendars, organizing meetings, and coordinating appointments. Candidates should become familiar with scheduling software and tools, such as Microsoft Outlook or Google Calendar, which can streamline these processes and help prevent scheduling conflicts. Effective time management skills are essential, as clerical roles often involve juggling multiple tasks and priorities. Developing a system for prioritizing tasks, setting deadlines, and allocating time efficiently can ensure that work is completed on schedule.

In addition to these core tasks, clerical roles often involve providing administrative support to colleagues and supervisors. This can include preparing meeting materials, organizing travel arrangements, and assisting with project coordination. Candidates should be prepared to take initiative, anticipate the needs of their team, and adapt to changing circumstances. Strong organizational skills, attention to detail, and a proactive attitude are essential in fulfilling these responsibilities effectively.

Understanding office equipment and technology is another important aspect of clerical work. Candidates should become proficient in using common office equipment, such as printers, copiers, and scanners, as well as software applications like word processors, spreadsheets, and presentation tools. Familiarity with these tools enhances productivity and allows candidates to troubleshoot minor issues independently, reducing downtime and ensuring smooth operations.

Problem-solving and critical thinking skills are invaluable in clerical roles, as unexpected challenges and issues often arise. Whether it's resolving a scheduling conflict, finding a missing document, or addressing a technical issue, the ability to think on one's feet and find effective solutions is crucial. Candidates should practice analyzing problems, considering potential solutions, and making informed decisions to develop these skills.

Ethical considerations and confidentiality are also important aspects of clerical work, particularly in the public sector. Candidates must understand the importance of maintaining confidentiality and handling sensitive information with care. This includes adhering to organizational policies and procedures, as well as relevant legal and regulatory requirements. Demonstrating integrity and professionalism in all aspects of clerical work is essential for building trust and maintaining the organization's reputation.

Filing and Record Management

Filing and record management are fundamental aspects of office practices, particularly in the civil service, where the organization and maintenance of documents are crucial for efficient operations. These tasks ensure that information is readily accessible, secure, and up-to-date, enabling public service employees to perform their duties effectively and maintain transparency and accountability.

A well-structured filing system is the backbone of effective record management. It involves categorizing, storing, and retrieving documents in a manner that is logical and easy to navigate. Common filing systems include alphabetical, numerical, and subject-based methods. Each system has its advantages and is chosen based on the type of documents being managed and the specific needs of the organization. For instance, alphabetical filing is often used for client records, while numerical systems may be more suited for documents like invoices and purchase orders. Subject-based filing is ideal for organizing information related to specific projects or topics.

In the digital age, electronic document management systems (EDMS) have become an integral part of filing and record management. EDMS allows for the storage, retrieval, and management of documents in digital format, offering numerous benefits over traditional paper-based systems. These include enhanced accessibility, improved security, and reduced physical storage requirements. Familiarity with EDMS is essential for candidates preparing for the civil service exam, as many public sector organizations have adopted these systems to streamline their operations.

When managing records, accuracy and attention to detail are paramount. Ensuring that documents are correctly labeled, categorized, and filed prevents misplacement and loss, which can lead to inefficiencies and potential legal or regulatory issues. Regular audits of filing systems help maintain their integrity, allowing for the identification and rectification of any discrepancies or errors. Candidates should practice meticulous record-keeping, developing habits that ensure documents are consistently and accurately managed.

Retention policies are a critical component of record management, dictating how long documents should be kept before they are disposed of or archived. These policies are often governed by legal or regulatory requirements and vary depending on the type of document. For example, financial records may need to be retained for several years for audit purposes, while personnel records might have different retention timelines. Understanding and adhering to retention policies ensures compliance with relevant laws and regulations and prevents the unnecessary accumulation of outdated documents.

Security is another vital aspect of filing and record management. Protecting sensitive information from unauthorized access, loss, or damage is crucial, particularly in the public sector, where data breaches can have significant consequences. Implementing security measures such as access controls, encryption, and regular backups helps safeguard documents and maintain their confidentiality and integrity. Candidates should become familiar with best practices for document security, ensuring they can contribute to a secure and compliant record management system.

The transition from paper-based to digital records presents its own set of challenges and opportunities. While digitization offers advantages such as increased accessibility and reduced storage space, it also requires careful planning and execution to ensure a smooth transition. This includes scanning and converting existing paper documents into digital format, organizing them within the EDMS, and training employees to use the new system effectively. Candidates should understand the processes involved in digitization and be prepared to adapt to changing technologies in the workplace.

Effective record management also involves the regular review and updating of documents to ensure they remain current and relevant. This includes revising policies, procedures, and other documents as necessary to reflect changes in laws, regulations, or organizational practices. Regular updates help maintain the accuracy and usefulness of records, supporting informed decision-making and efficient operations.

Communication plays a crucial role in filing and record management. Clear and consistent communication ensures that all employees understand the filing system, retention policies, and security measures in place. This includes providing training and resources to support employees in fulfilling their record management responsibilities. Candidates should develop strong communication skills, enabling them to convey information effectively and facilitate collaboration within their teams.

Office Equipment Proficiency

Office equipment proficiency is an indispensable skill for candidates preparing for the civil service exam, as it is integral to the efficient functioning of any public service office. Mastery of various office tools not only enhances productivity but also ensures that tasks are completed accurately and efficiently, contributing to the smooth operation of the organization.

Understanding the functionality and operation of essential office equipment is the first step toward proficiency. Printers, copiers, scanners, and fax machines are staples in most office environments. Each device has its specific functions and features, and becoming familiar with these can prevent common pitfalls and increase efficiency. For instance, knowing how to clear a paper jam in a printer or adjust settings on a copier can save valuable time and reduce frustration.

Printers and copiers, often multifunctional, serve not only to print and copy documents but also to scan and sometimes fax. Understanding how to operate these machines, including selecting appropriate settings for different tasks, is crucial. For example, choosing the correct paper size, print quality, or duplex printing can significantly impact the quality and professionalism of the final document. Regularly changing toner or ink cartridges and performing routine maintenance checks can prolong the life of these machines and minimize downtime.

Scanners are invaluable for digitizing documents, allowing for easy storage, retrieval, and sharing of information. Proficiency with scanners includes understanding how to adjust resolution settings for different types of documents, such as text versus images, and how to save files in various formats like PDF or JPEG. Familiarity with optical character recognition (OCR) software, which converts scanned images of text into editable text files, can further enhance the utility of scanned documents and streamline workflows.

Fax machines, though less common in the digital age, still hold relevance in certain sectors for their ability to send and receive documents quickly and securely. Understanding the basic operation of a fax machine, including how to send and receive faxes, manage fax numbers, and troubleshoot common issues, ensures that candidates can handle this task efficiently when required.

In addition to these traditional office machines, candidates should develop proficiency with modern digital tools and software applications. Word processors, spreadsheets, and presentation software are essential for creating, editing, and sharing documents and data. Mastery of these tools includes not only basic functions but also advanced features that can enhance productivity. For example, using templates in word processors can save time and ensure consistency, while advanced spreadsheet functions like pivot tables and macros can simplify data analysis and reporting.

Email and communication tools are vital for efficient office operations, facilitating internal and external communication. Proficiency with email clients involves more than sending and receiving messages; it includes organizing emails into folders, setting up filters to manage incoming messages, and understanding features like calendar integration for scheduling meetings. Additionally, familiarity with communication platforms such as video conferencing tools and instant messaging applications can enhance team collaboration and communication.

Office equipment proficiency also extends to understanding the security and maintenance of these tools. Regular updates to software and firmware ensure that devices operate efficiently and securely. Implementing security measures, such as password protection and data encryption, helps safeguard sensitive information and prevent unauthorized access. Candidates should be aware of these practices and understand their importance in maintaining the integrity and security of office operations.

Troubleshooting is an essential skill in managing office equipment, as technical issues can arise unexpectedly and disrupt workflow. Developing a systematic approach to problem-solving, such as identifying the issue, consulting manuals or online resources, and applying logical solutions, can resolve many common problems quickly. Knowing when to escalate an issue to technical support is also crucial, ensuring that more complex problems are addressed promptly and professionally.

For candidates aiming to excel in office roles, continuous learning and adaptation to new technologies are vital. Engaging with training resources, seeking opportunities to learn about new tools and equipment, and staying informed about industry trends can enhance skills and knowledge. This commitment to professional development ensures that candidates remain competitive and effective in their roles, adapting to the evolving demands of the workplace.

Customer Service and Communication

Customer service and communication are pivotal elements of office practices, especially within the civil service, where interactions with the public and colleagues are frequent and varied. Mastery of these skills ensures that candidates can provide high-quality service, foster positive relationships, and contribute to the effective functioning of their organization.

Effective customer service begins with understanding the needs and expectations of the client, whether they are internal colleagues or external members of the public. This requires a blend of empathy, patience, and active listening. When engaging with clients, it is crucial to listen attentively, acknowledging their concerns and demonstrating an understanding of their situation. This not only builds trust but also provides the foundation for resolving issues effectively.

Communication skills are the bedrock of customer service, involving both verbal and non verbal elements. Clarity and professionalism in verbal communication are essential, whether it's through phone calls, in-person interactions, or virtual meetings. Using clear, concise language helps prevent misunderstandings and ensures that the client receives the necessary information. Non-verbal communication, such as body language, facial expressions, and eye contact, also plays a significant role in conveying openness and attentiveness.

Written communication is equally important, encompassing emails, letters, reports, and memos. These communications should be clear, concise, and free of errors, reflecting a professional image of the organization. Crafting effective written communication involves structuring information logically, maintaining a formal tone, and using appropriate grammar and punctuation. Proofreading is a critical step in this process, ensuring that the final document is polished and error-free.

Building rapport with clients is a key aspect of customer service, fostering a sense of trust and cooperation. This involves being personable, approachable, and respectful in all interactions. Small gestures, such as using the client's name, displaying a positive attitude, and expressing gratitude, can significantly enhance the client's experience and perception of the organization. Rapport-building is particularly important in situations where clients may be frustrated or upset, as it helps to diffuse tension and create a more positive environment for resolving issues.

Problem-solving skills are integral to customer service, as employees often encounter challenging situations that require quick thinking and effective solutions. This involves analyzing the situation, identifying potential solutions, and implementing the most appropriate one. Flexibility and adaptability are essential, as each client and situation is unique, requiring tailored approaches. Collaborating with colleagues or escalating issues to supervisors when necessary ensures that clients receive the support they need.

Time management is a crucial aspect of customer service, as employees must balance the needs of multiple clients while completing their other responsibilities. Prioritizing tasks, setting realistic deadlines, and managing client expectations are vital for maintaining efficiency and delivering timely service. Techniques such as creating to-do lists, using digital calendars, and setting reminders can help employees stay organized and focused on their tasks.

Feedback and continuous improvement are important elements of customer service, providing opportunities for growth and development. Soliciting feedback from clients and colleagues helps identify areas for improvement and reinforces positive behaviors. Constructive feedback should be viewed as an opportunity to learn and enhance skills, contributing to personal and professional growth. Engaging in regular training and development programs can further enhance customer service skills, ensuring that employees remain effective and competitive in their roles.

Cultural awareness and sensitivity are increasingly important in customer service, particularly in diverse environments. Understanding and respecting cultural differences in communication styles, social norms, and expectations can enhance interactions with clients from various backgrounds. This involves being open-minded, avoiding assumptions, and demonstrating respect for diverse perspectives. Employees should be aware of any organizational policies or training programs related to cultural competence and actively seek opportunities to expand their knowledge and skills in this area.

Technology plays a significant role in modern customer service, offering tools and platforms that enhance communication and streamline processes. Familiarity with customer relationship management (CRM) software, email clients, and communication platforms can improve efficiency and organization. These tools enable employees to track client interactions, manage inquiries, and access information quickly, enhancing the overall customer experience.

CHAPTER 6

STRATEGIC TEST-TAKING TECHNIQUES

Managing Test Anxiety

Time management skills are a cornerstone of success in any civil service role, where the ability to effectively prioritize tasks and manage time efficiently can significantly enhance productivity and job performance. The demands of public service often involve juggling multiple responsibilities, deadlines, and unexpected challenges, making time management an essential skill for candidates preparing for the civil service exam.

The first step in mastering time management is understanding the importance of setting clear goals and objectives. Having a roadmap helps prioritize tasks and allocate time effectively. Short-term and long-term goals should be realistic, measurable, and aligned with the broader objectives of the organization. Breaking down larger projects into smaller, manageable tasks can make them less overwhelming and easier to tackle, creating a clear path to completion.

Prioritization is a key component of time management, requiring individuals to assess the importance and urgency of tasks. The Eisenhower Box, a time management tool that categorizes tasks by urgency and importance, can be particularly useful for this purpose. By distinguishing between tasks that are urgent and important, individuals can focus on what truly matters and avoid getting sidetracked by less critical activities. This approach helps ensure that time and energy are directed toward tasks that align with organizational goals and deliver the most value.

Effective scheduling is another essential element of time management. Creating a daily or weekly schedule helps structure the day and allocate time for specific tasks, meetings, and breaks. Digital calendars and planning tools can aid in this process, offering reminders and alerts to keep individuals on track. When scheduling tasks, it's important to allocate sufficient time for each activity, allowing for potential disruptions and ensuring that deadlines are met without unnecessary stress.

Delegation is a powerful time management strategy that involves assigning tasks to others to free up time for higher-priority activities. Understanding when and how to delegate tasks is crucial, as it allows individuals to focus on their core responsibilities while empowering team members to contribute effectively. Clear communication and providing adequate resources and support are essential for successful delegation, ensuring that tasks are completed to the required standard.

Minimizing distractions is a vital aspect of managing time effectively. In today's digital age, constant notifications, emails, and social media can easily derail focus and productivity. Identifying common distractions and implementing strategies to reduce their impact is essential. This might involve setting specific times to check emails, turning off non-essential notifications, or creating a designated workspace that minimizes interruptions. By creating an environment conducive to focus and concentration, individuals can enhance their productivity and make the most of their available time.

Time management also involves recognizing the importance of breaks and downtime. While it may seem counterintuitive, taking regular breaks can actually improve productivity and prevent burnout. Short breaks throughout the day can help refresh the mind, boost concentration, and maintain energy levels. Techniques such as the Pomodoro Technique, which involves focused work sessions followed by short breaks, can be particularly effective for maintaining productivity and preventing fatigue.

Reflecting on and assessing time management practices is crucial for continuous improvement. Regularly reviewing how time is spent, identifying areas for improvement, and making necessary adjustments can enhance efficiency and effectiveness. Keeping a time log or journal can provide valuable insights into time usage patterns and highlight opportunities for optimization. By identifying tasks that take longer than expected or recurring time-wasting activities, individuals can make informed decisions about how to adjust their approach and improve their time management skills.

Technology can be a valuable ally in time management, offering tools and applications that streamline processes and enhance efficiency. Project management software, task management apps, and digital calendars can help organize tasks, set reminders, and track progress. Familiarity with these tools and their features can significantly improve time management capabilities, allowing individuals to automate routine tasks and focus on more strategic activities.

Time Allocation and Prioritization

Test anxiety is a common challenge faced by candidates preparing for the civil service exam. It can manifest as a range of physical and psychological symptoms, from increased heart rate and sweating to feelings of dread and negative self-talk. While a certain level of stress can be motivating, excessive anxiety can hinder performance and prevent candidates from showcasing their true abilities. Managing test anxiety is therefore essential for achieving success and demonstrating one's full potential.

Understanding the root causes of test anxiety is the first step in managing it effectively. Anxiety often stems from fear of failure, lack of preparation, or high personal expectations. Recognizing these factors allows candidates to address them directly and implement strategies to reduce their impact. For example, if fear of failure is a primary concern, reframing the exam as an opportunity to learn and grow, rather than a definitive measure of worth, can help alleviate pressure.

Preparation is a powerful antidote to test anxiety. Developing a comprehensive study plan that includes reviewing material, practicing test questions, and setting achievable goals can boost confidence and reduce uncertainty. Breaking study sessions into manageable chunks and incorporating regular breaks can enhance focus and prevent burnout. Additionally, simulating test conditions during practice sessions can help candidates become accustomed to the exam environment, making the actual test feel more familiar and less intimidating.

Mindfulness and relaxation techniques are effective tools for managing anxiety and promoting a sense of calm. Practices such as deep breathing, progressive muscle relaxation, and visualization can help candidates center themselves and reduce tension. Deep breathing involves taking slow, controlled breaths to regulate the body's physiological response to stress. Progressive muscle relaxation focuses on tensing and then releasing different muscle groups, helping to ease physical tension. Visualization techniques involve imagining a calm, peaceful scene or visualizing oneself successfully completing the exam, fostering a positive mindset.

Cognitive restructuring is another valuable strategy for managing test anxiety. This involves identifying and challenging negative thought patterns that contribute to anxiety, such as catastrophizing or engaging in all-or-nothing thinking. By replacing negative thoughts with more balanced and realistic ones, candidates can reduce anxiety and build self-confidence. For instance, instead of thinking, "I'll never be able to pass this exam," candidates can reframe it as, "I have prepared thoroughly, and I will do my best."

Time management during the exam is crucial for minimizing anxiety and maximizing performance. Prioritizing questions, allocating time effectively, and knowing when to move on from challenging questions can help candidates maintain focus and avoid feeling overwhelmed. If uncertainty arises, making an educated guess and marking the question for review later can prevent candidates from getting stuck and losing valuable time.

Support from peers, mentors, and family can provide encouragement and reinforce positive self-beliefs. Talking to others who have successfully navigated similar exams can offer practical advice and reassurance. Study groups can also provide a collaborative environment for sharing strategies and motivating one another. Having a support network fosters a sense of community and reminds candidates that they are not alone in their journey.

Lifestyle factors play a significant role in managing test anxiety. Ensuring adequate sleep, maintaining a balanced diet, and engaging in regular physical activity can improve overall well-being and resilience to stress. Sleep is particularly important, as it consolidates memory and enhances cognitive function. Candidates should prioritize getting enough rest in the days leading up to the exam to ensure they are alert and focused.

On the day of the exam, candidates can employ specific strategies to manage anxiety and optimize performance. Arriving early to the test center allows time to settle in, gather materials, and mentally prepare. Engaging in a brief relaxation exercise, such as deep breathing, before beginning the exam can help calm nerves and focus the mind. Positive self-talk, such as affirmations like "I am prepared and capable," can reinforce confidence and counteract self-doubt.

Post-exam reflection is an opportunity to evaluate what strategies worked well and identify areas for improvement. This reflection should be approached with a growth mindset, focusing on learning from the experience rather than dwelling on perceived failures. Constructive feedback from practice exams and self-assessment can guide future study efforts and enhance test-taking skills.

Answering Multiple Choice Questions

Navigating multiple choice questions on the civil service exam requires both strategy and precision. These questions can test a breadth of knowledge across various subjects, demanding not only familiarity with content but also the ability to effectively analyze and deduce the correct answers from the given options. Mastering this skill involves a combination of preparation, strategic thinking, and attention to detail.

A solid foundation of knowledge is essential for tackling multiple choice questions with confidence. This begins with a comprehensive study plan that covers all relevant topics and emphasizes understanding over rote memorization. Engaging with a variety of resources, such as textbooks, online courses, and practice tests, can provide a well-rounded perspective on the material. Regular review sessions help reinforce this knowledge, ensuring that key concepts are retained and easily recalled during the exam.

When approaching a multiple choice question, it is important to read the question stem carefully before considering the answer choices. Understanding what the question is asking is crucial, as it sets the stage for identifying the correct response. Pay close attention to keywords or phrases that may indicate the type of response required, and be mindful of qualifiers such as "always," "never," or "except," which can significantly alter the meaning of the question.

After thoroughly reading the question, attempt to answer it in your mind before reviewing the given options. This approach helps focus your thinking and may lead you to the correct answer without being influenced by distractor choices. Once you have a preliminary answer in mind, evaluate each of the provided options, systematically eliminating those that are clearly incorrect. This process of elimination can narrow down the choices and increase the likelihood of selecting the correct answer, even if you are unsure at first.

Distractors in multiple choice questions are designed to mislead or confuse. They may include options that are partially correct, contain common misconceptions, or are factually incorrect but plausible. Careful consideration of each option is necessary to identify these distractors and avoid being swayed by them. Comparing the remaining choices to your initial answer can provide clarity and confidence in your selection.

Time management is essential when answering multiple choice questions, as spending too long on any single question can detract from the time available for others. Establishing a pace that allows for a thorough reading of each question and evaluation of the options is critical. If a question proves particularly challenging, it can be beneficial to make an educated guess, mark it for review, and move on. Revisiting marked questions later can provide a fresh perspective and may lead to a clearer understanding after addressing other parts of the exam.

Educated guessing is a valuable technique when uncertainty arises. By eliminating obviously incorrect options, the odds of selecting the correct answer increase. In situations where all remaining choices seem plausible, selecting the option that most closely aligns with your initial understanding or intuition can often yield positive results.

Understanding the scoring system of the exam can also inform your approach to guessing. If there are no penalties for incorrect answers, guessing provides an opportunity to potentially increase your score without the risk of losing points. Conversely, if penalties exist, a more cautious approach may be warranted, focusing on eliminating as many incorrect options as possible before making a guess.

Regular practice with multiple choice questions is crucial for honing your skills and building confidence. Practice exams and question banks offer opportunities to apply strategies and identify areas that require further study. Reviewing explanations for both correct and incorrect answers is invaluable, as it highlights patterns in reasoning and helps develop the ability to quickly recognize correct answers during the actual exam.

Staying calm and focused during the exam is vital for maintaining clarity and making sound decisions. Anxiety can cloud judgment and lead to hasty or poorly considered choices. Techniques such as deep breathing, positive visualization, and affirmations can help maintain a steady mindset, allowing you to concentrate fully on each question.

Handling Unfamiliar Questions

Unfamiliar questions can pose a significant challenge during the civil service exam, often leaving candidates feeling unsure and apprehensive. However, these questions also provide an opportunity to demonstrate critical thinking and adaptability—skills that are highly valued in public service roles. Effective strategies for handling unfamiliar questions can make a considerable difference in overall performance and confidence.

The first step in addressing unfamiliar questions is to remain calm and composed. Anxiety can cloud judgment and hinder the ability to think clearly, making it essential to maintain a steady mindset. Taking a deep breath and reminding yourself of your preparation can help reduce stress and create mental space for problem-solving.

Careful reading and comprehension are crucial when faced with an unfamiliar question. Break down the question into its components, identify key terms, and determine what is being asked. This process can often reveal underlying concepts or connections to known material, making the question more approachable. Paying attention to detail is critical, as subtle cues in the wording can provide hints or context that guide your thought process.

Next, draw upon your existing knowledge base to make connections. Even if the question is not directly related to familiar topics, it may involve concepts or principles that you have encountered before. Consider how these elements might relate to the question at hand and use them as a starting point for developing an answer. This approach often involves looking for parallels between the unfamiliar content and similar ideas you have studied.

Logical reasoning and deduction play a significant role in handling unfamiliar questions. Analyze the information provided and use logical steps to eliminate implausible answers or solutions. For multiple-choice questions, this might involve ruling out options that are clearly incorrect or do not fit with the given data. For open-ended questions, consider different perspectives or approaches, and apply reasoning to construct a coherent response.

When dealing with questions that seem entirely foreign, educated guessing can be a valuable technique. This involves using any available information, however limited, to make an informed choice. Even if you are unsure of the correct answer, narrowing down the possibilities increases the likelihood of selecting the right one. Trusting your instincts and making a reasoned guess is often better than leaving the question unanswered, especially when there is no penalty for incorrect answers.

Analyzing Common Mistakes

Understanding and analyzing common mistakes made during the civil service exam is an invaluable part of preparation, offering insights that can be used to refine strategies and improve performance. Mistakes provide a learning opportunity, allowing candidates to identify areas of vulnerability and develop targeted approaches to overcome them. By addressing these common pitfalls, candidates can enhance their test-taking skills and boost their confidence.

One prevalent mistake is the misinterpretation of questions, often due to haste or anxiety. Candidates may rush through a question, missing crucial keywords or details that define the correct answer. To counteract this, it is essential to cultivate a habit of reading each question thoroughly and carefully. Taking a moment to break down the question, highlighting key terms, and ensuring a clear understanding of what is being asked can significantly reduce errors.

Another common error involves poor time management, leading to incomplete sections or rushed answers. Candidates may spend too long on challenging questions, leaving insufficient time for others. Establishing a clear plan for time allocation is critical. Practicing with timed exams helps develop a sense of pacing, allowing candidates to allocate time appropriately across different sections. Prioritizing questions based on difficulty and familiarity can also help maintain a steady flow and ensure that all questions are addressed within the allotted time.

Neglecting to review answers is a mistake that can cost valuable points. Under exam conditions, it is easy to make simple errors, such as misreading a question or miscalculating an answer. Allocating time at the end of the exam to review answers provides an opportunity to catch and correct these mistakes. During this review, it is helpful to revisit marked questions, ensuring that they have been answered to the best of one's ability.

Overconfidence can lead to errors, as candidates may assume they know the answer without fully considering all options. This is particularly true for multiple choice questions, where distractors are designed to appear plausible. Developing a disciplined approach to evaluating each option, even when the answer seems obvious, can prevent overconfidence from leading to mistakes. It is important to remain vigilant and methodical, ensuring that each choice is given due consideration.

Conversely, lack of confidence can also result in mistakes, often manifesting as second-guessing or changing answers unnecessarily. While reviewing answers is important, excessive changes based on doubt can backfire. Trusting one's initial instincts, especially when they are based on solid reasoning and knowledge, is often the best course of action. Building confidence through practice and preparation can help reduce the tendency to second-guess.

A failure to connect questions to broader concepts or patterns is another frequent issue. Exams often test not just rote memorization but the ability to apply knowledge to different contexts. Strengthening critical thinking skills and the ability to draw connections between topics can mitigate this issue. Engaging with practice questions that require application of knowledge in novel situations can help develop this skill, making it easier to see the underlying concepts during the actual exam.

Inadequate preparation is an overarching cause of many mistakes, stemming from a superficial understanding of the material. Comprehensive preparation includes not only studying content but also practicing with real exam questions and learning from mistakes made during practice. Reviewing incorrect answers to understand why they were wrong and what the correct answer should have been is crucial for deepening understanding and preventing similar errors in the future.

External distractions, both mental and environmental, can lead to mistakes during the exam. It is important to create a focused and conducive testing environment, minimizing distractions as much as possible. Mentally, techniques such as mindfulness and concentration exercises can help maintain focus and keep the mind from wandering. Being fully present and engaged with the exam material helps ensure that mistakes are minimized.

Finally, the pressure to perform can lead to anxiety-related mistakes, where stress impacts decision-making and clarity of thought. Developing effective stress management techniques, such as deep breathing, visualization, or positive self-talk, can help maintain a calm and focused state during the exam. Confidence in one's preparation and abilities also plays a crucial role in reducing anxiety and its associated mistakes.

Reviewing and Checking Answers

Thoroughly reviewing and checking answers is a vital component of a successful strategy for navigating the civil service exam. This phase of the test-taking process is often underestimated or rushed, yet it holds the potential to significantly improve scores and showcase the candidate's true capabilities. With a focus on precision and attention to detail, reviewing and checking answers can transform potential errors into opportunities for correction and clarity.

When the exam timer is ticking down, it can be tempting to submit your work and breathe a sigh of relief. However, allocating time for a meticulous review phase is crucial. The first step in this process involves managing your exam time wisely so that a buffer is available for review. Ideally, candidates should aim to complete the initial round of answering with enough time left to revisit each section. This buffer allows for a comprehensive review without the pressure of looming time constraints.

Approach the review process with a clear and focused mind. It's beneficial to start by taking a brief mental pause; a few deep breaths can help clear the mind and reset focus. This momentary pause is particularly useful for calming nerves and preparing to reassess your work with fresh eyes. Approach your answers with a critical yet constructive mindset, seeking out areas where clarity and precision can be improved.

Begin the review by revisiting questions that were flagged or marked during the initial answering phase. These are typically questions that presented uncertainty or required additional thought. Re-evaluating these questions with a calmer mind can provide new insights or a clearer perspective. Sometimes, stepping away from a problem and returning to it later can illuminate the answer or reveal a previously overlooked detail.

For multiple-choice sections, scrutinize each question to ensure that your selected answer aligns with your understanding of the question stem. Pay attention to the nuances of language used in both the question and the answer choices. Look for absolutes or qualifiers that might change the meaning, such as "always," "never," or "only." These words can significantly influence which option is correct. If you find discrepancies between your initial reasoning and the available choices, reassess your logic and adjust your answer if necessary.

In sections requiring written responses, such as essays or short answers, review your work for clarity, coherence, and completeness. Ensure that each response directly addresses the question asked and that your arguments or explanations are logically structured. Check for grammatical accuracy and the use of precise language, as these factors contribute to the clarity and professionalism of your response. A coherent and well-structured answer not only reflects your knowledge but also showcases your ability to communicate effectively.

Check calculations in quantitative sections carefully. Errors in arithmetic or misinterpretation of data can lead to incorrect conclusions. Rework calculations step-by-step if time permits, comparing your process and results to ensure consistency. Simple mistakes in computation are common under pressure, but they are often easily corrected upon review.

Avoid the impulse to change answers arbitrarily. While reviewing may lead to necessary corrections, frequent changes based on doubt rather than logic can be counterproductive. Trust your initial instincts unless there is a clear reason to believe a mistake was made. Overthinking can sometimes introduce errors rather than resolve them, so balance confidence with caution.

Utilize any remaining time to conduct a final sweep of the entire exam. Look for any unanswered questions or incomplete sections, ensuring that every part of the exam has been addressed to the best of your ability. A thorough final check also involves verifying that you have followed all instructions, such as correctly filling in answer sheets or adhering to word limits in written responses.

CHAPTER 7

PRACTICE TESTS AND DETAILED EXPLANATIONS

Full-Length Practice Test 1 (170 Q&A and Explanations)

Numerator:

- The whole number that appears on the top of a fraction.
- The figure beneath a fraction line.
- A decimal form of a fraction.
- The number that divides another.

Correct Answer: The whole number that appears on the top of a fraction.

Explanation: The numerator indicates how many parts of the whole are being considered in a fraction.

Denominator:

- The number that appears on the bottom of the fraction.
- The top number in a fraction.
- A number that represents a fraction's negative value.
- The part of a fraction that multiplies the numerator.

Correct Answer: The number that appears on the bottom of the fraction.

Explanation: The denominator signifies the total number of equal parts into which the whole is divided.

Proper Fraction:

- The numerator is smaller than the denominator.
- The numerator equals the denominator.
- The numerator is larger than the denominator.
- The fraction represents a whole number.

Correct Answer: The numerator is smaller than the denominator.

Explanation: In a proper fraction, the value is less than one, indicating that the parts considered are fewer than the total parts.

Improper Fraction:

- The numerator is larger than the denominator.
- The numerator equals the denominator.
- The numerator is smaller than the denominator.
- The fraction represents a proper fraction.

Correct Answer: The numerator is larger than the denominator.

Explanation: An improper fraction represents a value greater than one, where the parts considered exceed the total parts.

Mixed Numbers:

- A mixed number consists of a whole number and a proper fraction. An improper fraction can be written into a mixed number.

- A mixed number is always a fraction.

- A mixed number consists of two fractions.

- A mixed number is a negative value.

Correct Answer: A mixed number consists of a whole number and a proper fraction. An improper fraction can be written into a mixed number.

Explanation: Mixed numbers express quantities greater than one by combining a whole number with a fractional component.

Converting an Improper Fraction into a Mixed Number:

- Divide the numerator by the denominator. The result will be a whole number, with or without a remainder. Write the whole number. If there is a remainder, write a fraction with the remainder in the numerator and the original denominator in the denominator.

- Add the numerator to the denominator.

- Subtract the denominator from the numerator.

- Multiply the numerator by the denominator.

Correct Answer: Divide the numerator by the denominator. The result will be a whole number, with or without a remainder. Write the whole number. If there is a remainder, write a fraction with the remainder in the numerator and the original denominator in the denominator.

Explanation: This method breaks down the improper fraction into whole parts and leftover parts, forming a mixed number.

Converting a Mixed Number into an Improper Fraction:

- Multiply the whole number in the mixed number by the denominator of the fraction. Add the result to the numerator of the fraction.

- Subtract the denominator from the numerator.

- Add the whole number to the numerator.

- Divide the numerator by the whole number.

Correct Answer: Multiply the whole number in the mixed number by the denominator of the fraction. Add the result to the numerator of the fraction.

Explanation: This conversion process compiles all parts into a single fraction, allowing for easier operations like multiplication and division.

When to Convert Mixed Numbers into Improper Fractions:

- Whenever you are asked to multiply or divide mixed numbers.

- Only when adding mixed numbers.

- Converting is unnecessary for any operation.

- Only when subtracting mixed numbers.

Correct Answer: Whenever you are asked to multiply or divide mixed numbers.

Explanation: Converting to improper fractions simplifies multiplication and division by treating all numbers uniformly.

Reducing a Fraction:

- You reduce a fraction by dividing both the numerator and the denominator by a single value that divides evenly into both of them.

- Multiply the numerator by the denominator.

- Subtract the denominator from the numerator.

- Add the numerator to the denominator.

Correct Answer: You reduce a fraction by dividing both the numerator and the denominator by a single value that divides evenly into both of them.

Explanation: Reducing a fraction simplifies it to its lowest terms, making calculations more manageable and results clearer.

Key Words for Equal:

- Is, are, has, was, were, had

- Sum, together, more, total

- Product, times, of

- Difference, less than, fewer

Correct Answer: Is, are, has, was, were, had

Explanation: These words indicate equality or equivalence in equations or statements.

Key Words for Addition:

- Sum, together, more, total, greater, or older than

- Product, times, of

- Difference, less than, fewer

- Per, evenly

Correct Answer: Sum, together, more, total, greater, or older than

Explanation: These words suggest combining values, indicating an addition operation.

Key Words for Multiplication:

- Product, times, of

- Sum, together, more

- Difference, less than, fewer

- Per, evenly

Correct Answer: Product, times, of

Explanation: These words are often used to describe multiplication operations, reflecting repeated addition.

Keywords for Division:

- Per, evenly

- Sum, together, more

- Product, times, of

- Difference, less than, fewer

Correct Answer: Per, evenly

Explanation: These terms imply dividing a quantity into equal parts, indicative of division.

Key Words for Subtraction:

- Difference, less than, fewer, or younger than, remain, left over

- Sum, together, more

- Product, times, of

- Per, evenly

Correct Answer: Difference, less than, fewer, or younger than, remain, left over

Explanation: These words are associated with taking away or comparing quantities, indicating subtraction.

Example of Key Words for Subtraction:

- Jacob has 5 fewer than Leslie.
- Jacob has 5 more than Leslie.
- Jacob has 5 times more than Leslie.
- Jacob shares 5 equally with Leslie.

Correct Answer: Jacob has 5 fewer than Leslie.

Explanation: This sentence indicates a subtraction situation where Jacob's quantity is less than Leslie's by five.

Key Words in Distance Formula Problems:

- speed, plane, train, boat, car, walk, run, climb, and swim
- calculate, subtract, add, divide
- numerator, denominator, fraction, remainder
- integer, decimal, percent, ratio

Correct Answer: speed, plane, train, boat, car, walk, run, climb, and swim

Explanation: These key words often indicate movement and are used to identify distance problems involving the distance formula.

Distance Formula:

- Rate x Time = Distance
- Distance / Time = Rate
- Time + Distance = Rate
- Rate - Time = Distance

Correct Answer: Rate x Time = Distance

Explanation: This formula calculates the distance traveled by multiplying the rate of speed by the time of travel.

Key Elements in the Distance Formula:

- rate, time, distance
- numerator, denominator, fraction
- addition, subtraction, multiplication
- speed, velocity, acceleration

Correct Answer: rate, time, distance

Explanation: These elements are the components needed to solve for distance, rate, or time in distance-related problems.

Solving Word Problems:

- Translate the problem into an algebraic equation and then solve for the missing information; work backwards by plugging in one of the answer choices.
- Estimate the answer based on intuition.

- Only use trial and error methods.
- Rely solely on calculator-based solutions.

Correct Answer: Translate the problem into an algebraic equation and then solve for the missing information; work backwards by plugging in one of the answer choices.

Explanation: These methods offer systematic approaches to solve word problems by creating equations or verifying solutions with given options.

Divisibility Trick for 3:

- Add all of its digits. If the sum of the digits is divisible by 3, the number itself is divisible by 3.
- Check if the number is even.
- Divide the number by 5 for verification.
- Ensure the number ends with 0 or 5.

Correct Answer: Add all of its digits. If the sum of the digits is divisible by 3, the number itself is divisible by 3.

Explanation: This shortcut simplifies checking a number's divisibility by 3, using a basic sum of digits.

Raising Fractions to Higher Terms:

- It allows you to rewrite a fraction with a larger numerator and denominator.
- Convert fractions to decimals.
- Simplify fractions to their lowest terms.
- Change fractions to whole numbers.

Correct Answer: It allows you to rewrite a fraction with a larger numerator and denominator.

Explanation: Raising fractions to higher terms standardizes them for addition or subtraction, aligning denominators.

Adding Fractions with Common Denominators:

- Simply just add the numerators and write the result over the denominator. Do not add the denominators.
- Add both numerators and denominators.
- Multiply the numerators and keep the denominators constant.
- Subtract denominators from numerators.

Correct Answer: Simply just add the numerators and write the result over the denominator. Do not add the denominators.

Explanation: This rule simplifies the process by maintaining a common denominator, focusing only on the numerators.

Adding Mixed Numbers:

- Add the whole numbers together, and then add the numerators together and place them over the denominators. Do not add the denominators.
- Only add whole numbers, ignoring fractions.
- Convert mixed numbers to improper fractions first.
- Subtract fractions from whole numbers.

Correct Answer: Add the whole numbers together, and then add the numerators together and place them over the denominators. Do not add the denominators.

Explanation: This method combines both whole and fractional parts, ensuring a complete addition of mixed numbers.

Improper Fraction Conversion:

- If the sum of the 2 fractions happens to be an improper fraction, you must convert the improper fraction into a mixed number.

- Keep improper fractions as they are.

- Improper fractions require no conversion.

- Only convert for subtraction operations.

Correct Answer: If the sum of the 2 fractions happens to be an improper fraction, you must convert the improper fraction into a mixed number.

Explanation: Converting to a mixed number provides a clearer representation of the total value.

Adding Fractions Without Common Denominators:

- You cannot add fractions unless it has a common denominator.

- Add numerators regardless of denominators.

- Multiply all denominators first.

- Subtract larger denominators from smaller ones.

Correct Answer: You cannot add fractions unless it has a common denominator.

Explanation: Common denominators are essential for ensuring accurate addition of fractional parts.

Finding a Common Denominator:

- Look at the denominators of all the fractions in the problem. Do they all divide evenly into the largest denominator? If they do, that number is your common denominator. If they don't, run through the multiplication table of the largest denominator until you find a number that all the other denominators divide into evenly.

- Subtract the smallest denominator from the largest.

- Multiply all denominators by each other.

- Divide the largest numerator by the smallest.

Correct Answer: Look at the denominators of all the fractions in the problem. Do they all divide evenly into the largest denominator? If they do, that number is your common denominator. If they don't, run through the multiplication table of the largest denominator until you find a number that all the other denominators divide into evenly.

Explanation: Finding a common denominator standardizes fractions, allowing for seamless addition or subtraction.

Subtracting Fractions:

- Subtracting fractions is just like adding them. When fractions share common denominators, simply subtract the numerators. Do not subtract the denominators.

- Subtract denominators from numerators.

- Convert to improper fractions before subtracting.

- Multiply numerators and subtract denominators.

Correct Answer: Subtracting fractions is just like adding them. When fractions share common denominators, simply subtract the numerators. Do not subtract the denominators.

Explanation: This maintains the common denominator, focusing only on the difference between numerators.

Subtracting Mixed Numbers:

- Subtract the whole number from the whole number and the fraction from the fraction.

- Convert mixed numbers to improper fractions first.

- Subtract fractions only, ignoring whole numbers.

- Add the numerators and subtract the denominators.

Correct Answer: Subtract the whole number from the whole number and the fraction from the fraction.

Explanation: This approach ensures both whole parts and fractional parts are accurately subtracted in mixed numbers.

Extra Steps in Subtracting Fractions:

- If the fraction in the second mixed number is larger than the fraction in the first mixed number, you will have to borrow in order to rewrite the first number.

- If the whole numbers are equal.

- When both fractions are proper.

- Only with improper fractions.

Correct Answer: If the fraction in the second mixed number is larger than the fraction in the first mixed number, you will have to borrow in order to rewrite the first number.

Explanation: This adjustment ensures that the subtraction does not result in a negative fraction by borrowing from the whole number part.

Subtraction Without Common Denominators:

- It's like adding fractions; you must find the common denominator.

- Subtract numerators directly.

- Multiply denominators together first.

- Divide numerators by denominators.

Correct Answer: It's like adding fractions; you must find the common denominator.

Explanation: Finding a common denominator aligns fractions for accurate subtraction.

Multiplying Fractions:

- Multiplying fractions is much easier than adding or subtracting. All you have to do is multiply the numerators and the denominators.

- Add numerators and denominators.

- Subtract denominators from numerators.

- Divide numerators by denominators.

Correct Answer: Multiplying fractions is much easier than adding or subtracting. All you have to do is multiply the numerators and the denominators.

Explanation: This straightforward method yields the product of two fractions by directly multiplying across.

Multiplying Mixed Numbers:

- Change any mixed numbers to an improper fraction; then multiply as normal.

- Convert to proper fractions before multiplying.

- Add fractions first.

- Multiply whole numbers only.

Correct Answer: Change any mixed numbers to an improper fraction; then multiply as normal.

Explanation: Converting to improper fractions simplifies multiplication, ensuring all parts are included.

Calculating Fans for the Home Team:

- To solve, multiply 8400 by 3/4
- Divide 8400 by 4
- Add 3/4 to 8400
- Subtract 3/4 from 8400

Correct Answer: To solve, multiply 8400 by 3/4

Explanation: Multiplying gives the portion of fans supporting the home team, using the fraction to find a part of the whole.

Dividing Fractions:

- Dividing fractions is just like multiplying fractions, but with one extra step. Use the reciprocal of the second fraction and turn the division sign into a multiplication sign.
- Add the fractions first.
- Subtract the numerators.
- Divide numerators by denominators.

Correct Answer: Dividing fractions is just like multiplying fractions, but with one extra step. Use the reciprocal of the second fraction and turn the division sign into a multiplication sign.

Explanation: This method effectively transforms division into multiplication, simplifying the process.

Dividing a Fraction by a Whole Number:

- First, change the whole number to a fraction by putting the whole number in the numerator of a fraction with a denominator of 1.
- Subtract the whole number from the fraction.
- Multiply the fraction by the whole number.
- Leave the fraction as it is.

Correct Answer: First, change the whole number to a fraction by putting the whole number in the numerator of a fraction with a denominator of 1.

Explanation: This conversion allows for straightforward multiplication, simplifying division by whole numbers.

Dividing Mixed Numbers:

- Rewrite them as improper fractions.
- Add whole numbers first.
- Subtract fractions from whole numbers.
- Convert to decimals.

Correct Answer: Rewrite them as improper fractions.

Explanation: Converting to improper fractions ensures all parts of the mixed numbers are included in the division.

Decimal Equivalents:

- 0.1 is 1 tenth, 1/10

- 0.01 is 1 tenth, 1/10
- 0.001 is 1 tenth, 1/10
- 0.0001 is 1 tenth, 1/10

Correct Answer: 0.1 is 1 tenth, 1/10

Explanation: This fraction represents a part of a whole, equivalent to the decimal provided.

Can Zero Be Added to the Right of a Decimal:

- Yes, .01 is the same value as .01000. This is helpful when adding, subtracting, or dividing by decimals.
- No, it changes the value.
- Only if the decimal is less than 0.1.
- Only in multiplication.

Correct Answer: Yes, .01 is the same value as .01000. This is helpful when adding, subtracting, or dividing by decimals.

Explanation: Adding zeros after the decimal does not change its value, maintaining equivalence, which aids in alignment for operations.

Mixed Decimal:

- A decimal with numbers on both sides of the decimal point.
- A decimal with numbers only on one side.
- A fraction expressed in decimal form.
- A number with no fractional part.

Correct Answer: A decimal with numbers on both sides of the decimal point.

Explanation: Mixed decimals include whole numbers and fractional parts, separated by a decimal point.

Decimals with Numbers to the Right Only:

- A decimal, not a mixed decimal.
- A mixed decimal.
- A whole number.
- A fraction.

Correct Answer: A decimal, not a mixed decimal.

Explanation: Such decimals represent only fractional parts, lacking whole numbers to the left of the decimal.

Writing a Fraction as a Decimal:

- Divide the numerator by the denominator.
- Multiply the numerator by 10.
- Add the numerator and denominator.
- Subtract the denominator from the numerator.

Correct Answer: Divide the numerator by the denominator.

Explanation: This division expresses the fraction as a decimal, illustrating the part of a whole numerically.

Changing a Decimal into a Fraction:

- Write the digits of the decimal as the numerator of a fraction and write the decimal's name as the denominator of the fraction. Reduce if possible.

- Multiply the decimal by 100.

- Add decimal places as zeros.

- Subtract decimal digits from whole numbers.

Correct Answer: Write the digits of the decimal as the numerator of a fraction and write the decimal's name as the denominator of the fraction. Reduce if possible.

Explanation: This method translates the decimal into a fraction form, reducing it for simplicity.

1/5 Converted to a Decimal:

- 0.2

- 0.25

- 0.5

- 0.75

Correct Answer: 0.2

Explanation: When dividing 1 by 5, the result is 0.2, representing one part of five.

1/4 Converted to a Decimal:

- 0.25

- 0.33

- 0.5

- 0.75

Correct Answer: 0.25

Explanation: Dividing 1 by 4 yields 0.25, denoting one quarter of a whole.

1/3 Converted to a Decimal:

- 0.33

- 0.25

- 0.5

- 0.75

Correct Answer: 0.33

Explanation: This division results in a repeating decimal, indicating a non-terminating cycle.

2/5 Converted to a Decimal:

- 0.4

- 0.25

- 0.5

- 0.75

Correct Answer: 0.4

Explanation: Two-fifths of a whole is represented as 0.4 in decimal form.

1/2 Converted to a Decimal:

- 0.5
- 0.25
- 0.75
- 0.33

Correct Answer: 0.5

Explanation: Dividing 1 by 2 results in 0.5, indicating half of a whole.

3/5 Converted to a Decimal:

- 0.6
- 0.25
- 0.5
- 0.75

Correct Answer: 0.6

Explanation: This conversion shows three-fifths as 0.6, a simple decimal form.

2/3 Converted to a Decimal:

- 0.66
- 0.25
- 0.5
- 0.75

Correct Answer: 0.66

Explanation: Two-thirds results in a repeating decimal, illustrating an ongoing sequence.

3/4 Converted to a Decimal:

- 0.75
- 0.25
- 0.5
- 0.33

Correct Answer: 0.75

Explanation: Three-quarters of a whole is expressed as 0.75, a straightforward conversion.

Bar Over the Last Digit in Some Decimals:

- It indicates that the decimal repeats infinitely. Decimals are not the most precise way to represent fractions whose denominators are not factors of a power of 10 (powers include 10; 100; 1000; 10000, etc.).
- It shows the decimal is exact.
- It marks the end of a decimal.
- It indicates rounding.

Correct Answer: It indicates that the decimal repeats infinitely. Decimals are not the most precise way to represent fractions whose denominators are not factors of a power of 10 (powers include 10; 100; 1000; 10000, etc.).

Explanation: The bar notation simplifies representation of repeating decimals, denoting endless cycles.

Comparing Decimals:

- Compare 0.08 and 0.1; when compared, 0.1 is the largest between the two.
- 0.08 is larger.
- Both are equal.
- Compare by subtracting.

Correct Answer: Compare 0.08 and 0.1; when compared, 0.1 is the largest between the two.

Explanation: Comparing decimals involves assessing place values, where 0.1 exceeds 0.08.

Percentages:

- The word percent comes from the Latin words meaning "for every one hundred." A percent expresses the relationship between a part and a whole in terms of 100.
- Percentages are less than 1.
- Percentages are always whole numbers.
- Percentages are fractions only.

Correct Answer: The word percent comes from the Latin words meaning "for every one hundred." A percent expresses the relationship between a part and a whole in terms of 100.

Explanation: Percentages relate parts to a base of 100, facilitating comparisons and calculations.

Changing a Percent to a Fraction:

- A percent can easily be written as a fraction. Simply take the percent and put it in the numerator of the fraction. Then, write 100 in the denominator.
- Add 100 to the numerator.
- Subtract the percent from 100.
- Multiply by 100.

Correct Answer: A percent can easily be written as a fraction. Simply take the percent and put it in the numerator of the fraction. Then, write 100 in the denominator.

Explanation: This conversion translates percentages into fractions, simplifying further calculations.

Example of Percent to Fraction Conversion:

- Convert 75% to a fraction: 75/100
- Convert 75% to a fraction: 75/10
- Convert 75% to a decimal: 0.75
- Convert 75% to a whole number: 75

Correct Answer: Convert 75% to a fraction: 75/100

Explanation: Placing 75 over 100 creates a fraction representing the percentage, which can be reduced or used directly.

Writing a Fraction as a Percent:

- Multiply the fraction by 100/1.
- Divide the fraction by 100.
- Add 100 to the fraction.

- Subtract 100 from the fraction.

Correct Answer: Multiply the fraction by 100/1.

Explanation: Multiplying by 100 converts the fraction to a percentage by scaling up its value to relate to a whole of 100.

Another Way to Convert a Fraction to a Decimal:

- Divide the numerator by the denominator, and then move the decimal point 2 places to the right in your quotient.
- Add 100 to the decimal.
- Subtract the denominator from the numerator.
- Multiply the decimal by 10.

Correct Answer: Divide the numerator by the denominator, and then move the decimal point 2 places to the right in your quotient.

Explanation: This method translates a fraction to decimal form before converting it to a percentage by adjusting the decimal point.

10% Converted to a Fraction:

- 1/10
- 1/5
- 1/4
- ½

Correct Answer: 1/10

Explanation: Moving from percentage to fraction involves placing the percent over 100, simplifying when possible.

20% Converted to a Fraction:

- 1/5
- 1/10
- 1/4
- ½

Correct Answer: 1/5

Explanation: This fraction represents 20 parts out of 100, simplified to one-fifth.

25% Converted to a Fraction:

- 1/4
- 1/5
- 1/10
- ½

Correct Answer: 1/4

Explanation: The percentage 25% corresponds to one-quarter when expressed as a fraction.

30% Converted to a Fraction:

- 3/10

- 1/4
- 1/5
- 1/3

Correct Answer: 3/10

Explanation: Thirty percent simplifies to three-tenths in fractional form.

33 1/3% Converted to a Fraction:

- 1/3
- 3/10
- 1/5
- ½

Correct Answer: 1/3

Explanation: This recurring percentage translates into one-third, a common fractional representation.

40% Converted to a Fraction:

- 2/5
- 1/4
- 1/5
- 3/10

Correct Answer: 2/5

Explanation: Forty percent simplifies to two-fifths, indicating a larger portion than the base.

50% Converted to a Fraction:

- 1/2
- 1/4
- 1/5
- 3/10

Correct Answer: 1/2

Explanation: This half represents an equal division of the whole, corresponding to 50%.

60% Converted to a Fraction:

- 3/5
- 1/2
- 1/4
- 2/5

Correct Answer: 3/5

Explanation: Sixty percent translates to three-fifths, indicating a substantial majority of the whole.

66 2/3% Converted to a Fraction:

- 2/3
- 1/2
- 1/3

- 3/5

Correct Answer: 2/3

Explanation: This fraction represents two-thirds, a repeating percentage value.

80% Converted to a Fraction:

- 4/5
- 2/3
- 1/2
- ¼

Correct Answer: 4/5

Explanation: Eighty percent simplifies to four-fifths, showing a high proportion of the whole.

100% Converted to a Fraction:

- 1/1 = 1
- 1/2
- 1/4
- 2/3

Correct Answer: 1/1 = 1

Explanation: One hundred percent equates to a whole, represented as one.

Changing a Percent to a Decimal:

- It's the same way as converting a decimal to a percent, but instead of moving the decimal point to the right 2 places, you move the % sign to the left 2 places and change the sign to a decimal.
- Add two zeros before the decimal.
- Subtract two digits from the numerator.
- Multiply by 100.

Correct Answer: It's the same way as converting a decimal to a percent, but instead of moving the decimal point to the right 2 places, you move the % sign to the left 2 places and change the sign to a decimal.

Explanation: This process shifts the percentage into decimal form, simplifying the representation.

Solving for % Word Problems:

- Solve by finding the percent of a whole, what percent one number is of another, or the whole when the percent of a number is given.
- Add percentages directly.
- Subtract the smaller percentage from the larger.
- Divide percentages by whole numbers.

Correct Answer: Solve by finding the percent of a whole, what percent one number is of another, or the whole when the percent of a number is given.

Explanation: These forms guide the approach to calculating percentages relative to quantities.

Example of Finding the Percent as a Whole:

- What is 30% of 40? Translates to 30/100 x 40 = 12

- $30/100 + 40 = 70$
- $40/30 = 1.333$
- Subtract 30 from 40.

Correct Answer: What is 30% of 40? Translates to $30/100 \times 40 = 12$

Explanation: Multiplying provides the portion of 40 that corresponds to 30%.

Example of Finding What Percent One Number is of Another:

- 12 is what percent of 40? Translates to $12 = x/100 \times 40$, solving gives $x = 30$
- $12 + 40 = 52$
- $40 - 12 = 28$
- $12 \times 40 = 480$

Correct Answer: 12 is what percent of 40? Translates to $12 = x/100 \times 40$, solving gives $x = 30$

Explanation: This equation calculates the percentage that 12 represents of 40.

Example of Finding the Whole When the % of a Number is Given:

- 12 is 30% of what number? Translates to $12 = 30/100 \times y$, solving gives $y = 40$
- $12 + 30 = 42$
- $30 - 12 = 18$
- $12 \times 30 = 360$

Correct Answer: 12 is 30% of what number? Translates to $12 = 30/100 \times y$, solving gives $y = 40$

Explanation: This method finds the original total amount from which a given percentage equals 12.

Techniques for Questions on Percent Increase and Decrease:

- Remember that after you calculate the percent, you must add (increase) or subtract (decrease) in order to determine the final result.
- Always increase percentages.
- Only subtract percentages.
- Ignore percentage changes.

Correct Answer: Remember that after you calculate the percent, you must add (increase) or subtract (decrease) in order to determine the final result.

Explanation: This technique ensures that changes in value are accurately computed, reflecting true adjustments.

Most Common Reading Comprehension Questions:

- Summarize the primary theme of the text.
- Identify specific details or facts within the text.
- Make inferences or conclusions based on the text.
- Define unusual vocabulary words found in the text.

Correct Answer: Summarize the primary theme of the text.

Explanation: The main idea captures the essence of the passage, providing a cohesive understanding of its overall message.

Main Idea of a Paragraph or Passage:

- Is what the paragraph or passage is mostly about.
- Lists all the details.
- Focuses on a single word.
- Describes the last sentence only.

Correct Answer: Is what the paragraph or passage is mostly about.

Explanation: Understanding the main idea involves grasping the central concept or theme that the passage predominantly discusses.

When Might a Main Idea Answer Be Incorrect?

- When the answer choice only applies to one detail or a small portion of the paragraph or passage.
- When it covers the entire passage.
- When it contains no details.
- When it's the first sentence.

Correct Answer: When the answer choice only applies to one detail or a small portion of the paragraph or passage.

Explanation: Focusing on a limited part of the text does not accurately represent the overarching main idea.

Topic Sentence:

- The sentence that expresses the main idea. Sometimes the answer to a main idea question is stated clearly in the passage, frequently found in the first or last sentence.
- Only appears at the end.
- Lists all supporting details.
- Is always in the second paragraph.

Correct Answer: The sentence that expresses the main idea. Sometimes the answer to a main idea question is stated clearly in the passage, frequently found in the first or last sentence.

Explanation: The topic sentence often provides a direct expression of the main idea, guiding the reader's understanding.

When the Main Idea Is Not Stated in the Topic Sentence:

- It is usually implied by the overall content of the passage. In such circumstances, you will need to deduce the main idea from the passage.
- It is never found.
- It is irrelevant.
- It is in the title.

Correct Answer: It is usually implied by the overall content of the passage. In such circumstances, you will need to deduce the main idea from the passage.

Explanation: Sometimes, understanding requires interpreting the passage's overall context to discern the main idea.

The Main Idea Describes:

- The entire passage or paragraph. If it only describes one part or one detail, it is not the correct answer.

- Only the introduction.
- Just the conclusion.
- A single sentence.

Correct Answer: The entire passage or paragraph. If it only describes one part or one detail, it is not the correct answer.

Explanation: The main idea should encapsulate the full scope of the passage's content and intent.

Just Because an Answer Refers to the Entire Passage:

- Doesn't mean that it is correct. Although such answers are usually correct, occasionally an incorrect answer will refer to the entire passage or paragraph.
- Means it is always correct.
- Indicates a summary.
- Confirms a detail.

Correct Answer: Doesn't mean that it is correct. Although such answers are usually correct, occasionally an incorrect answer will refer to the entire passage or paragraph.

Explanation: An incorrect interpretation may inaccurately represent the text, despite mentioning the entire passage.

What Makes an Answer Incorrect in a Main Idea Question?

- It describes the content in the passage or paragraph inaccurately. Most often, it states a position stronger than the one the writer takes.
- It agrees with the passage.
- It is the first choice.
- It summarizes the passage.

Correct Answer: It describes the content in the passage or paragraph inaccurately. Most often, it states a position stronger than the one the writer takes.

Explanation: Misrepresenting the passage's content or overstating an argument can lead to inaccurate conclusions.

Ensure the Main Idea Answer Accurately Describes:

- The content of the passage or paragraph.
- The title of the passage.
- The author's name.
- The last sentence.

Correct Answer: The content of the passage or paragraph.

Explanation: An accurate description of the main idea captures the essence and intent of the passage's content.

Detail Questions Ask You To Identify:

- A specific piece of information from the passage.
- The main idea.
- The author's opinion.
- The conclusion.

Correct Answer: A specific piece of information from the passage.

Explanation: Detail questions focus on retrieving precise facts or details explicitly stated within the text.

Detail Questions Usually Contain Phrases Like:

- According to the passage... / The passage states...
- Summarize the passage...
- The main idea is...
- The author believes...

Correct Answer: According to the passage... / The passage states...

Explanation: These phrases signal that the question seeks specific information directly from the text.

The Correct Answer to a Detail Question:

- Will be a direct quote or a paraphrase of information in the passage.
- Will summarize the passage.
- Will provide an opinion.
- Will restate the main idea.

Correct Answer: Will be a direct quote or a paraphrase of information in the passage.

Explanation: Accurate detail answers reflect the text's actual content, either verbatim or as a close paraphrase.

What Cannot Be the Correct Answer on a Detail Question?

- Any answer stating information that does not appear in the passage.
- An answer summarizing the passage.
- An answer providing an opinion.
- An answer agreeing with the passage.

Correct Answer: Any answer stating information that does not appear in the passage.

Explanation: For detail questions, correctness hinges on the presence of the information in the text.

Why Are Not All Answers That Repeat Information Necessarily Correct?

- The answer must also be relevant to the question being asked. Some incorrect answers will contain irrelevant information from the passage.
- They might be too detailed.
- They might be too brief.
- They might summarize the passage.

Correct Answer: The answer must also be relevant to the question being asked. Some incorrect answers will contain irrelevant information from the passage.

Explanation: Relevance is key; correct answers must directly address the question's focus.

Steps to Answer a Detail Question:

- First, read the question to determine its subject. Next, determine where in the passage the subject of the question is discussed. Reread the portion of the passage before answering.
- Summarize the passage.
- Guess based on the first sentence.
- Choose the longest answer.

Correct Answer: First, read the question to determine its subject. Next, determine where in the passage the subject of the question is discussed. Reread the portion of the passage before answering.

Explanation: This systematic approach ensures precision in locating and confirming specific details.

Inference Questions Ask You To:

- Find information in the paragraph, and then use it to draw an inference that is necessarily, or deductively, true.

- Summarize the paragraph.

- List all details.

- Provide an opinion.

Correct Answer: Find information in the paragraph, and then use it to draw an inference that is necessarily, or deductively, true.

Explanation: Inference questions require logical reasoning based on the text's given information.

Inference Questions Often Begin With:

- It can be inferred from the passage... / The passage suggests... / Which of the following conclusions is best supported...

- State the main idea...

- Provide a summary...

- Find a detail...

Correct Answer: It can be inferred from the passage... / The passage suggests... / Which of the following conclusions is best supported...

Explanation: These prompts guide readers to deduce deeper meanings or implications from the text.

When Answering an Inference Question:

- Do not choose an answer that requires you to make a major assumption or to use outside knowledge. Look for answers that are fully supported by information in the passage.

- Always make assumptions.

- Use personal opinions.

- Ignore the passage content.

Correct Answer: Do not choose an answer that requires you to make a major assumption or to use outside knowledge. Look for answers that are fully supported by information in the passage.

Explanation: Inferences should be grounded in the text, avoiding speculative leaps or external information.

Questions Testing Vocabulary:

- Are really trying to measure how well you can figure out the meaning of an unfamiliar word from its context.

- Test your memory.

- List synonyms.

- Provide definitions.

Correct Answer: Are really trying to measure how well you can figure out the meaning of an unfamiliar word from its context.

Explanation: Contextual clues help deduce meanings, showcasing comprehension skills.

Context Refers To:

- The words and ideas surrounding the vocabulary word.
- The main idea.
- The passage title.
- The author's biography.

Correct Answer: The words and ideas surrounding the vocabulary word.

Explanation: Context provides the necessary backdrop for understanding unfamiliar terms.

If the Context Is Clear Enough in a Vocabulary Question:

- You should be able to substitute a nonsense word for the one being sought and still be able to find the correct answer because you will be able to determine meaning strictly from the sense of the sentence.
- Always guess the meaning.
- Ignore the word.
- Use a dictionary.

Correct Answer: You should be able to substitute a nonsense word for the one being sought and still be able to find the correct answer because you will be able to determine meaning strictly from the sense of the sentence.

Explanation: Contextual understanding allows for identifying meaning without relying on the word itself.

The Tested Word Itself May Contain a Context Clue:

- Look for familiar prefixes and suffixes. Look to see if the word shares a common root with some other word you know.
- Ignore the word.
- Use only the sentence.
- Guess based on the first letter.

Correct Answer: Look for familiar prefixes and suffixes. Look to see if the word shares a common root with some other word you know.

Explanation: Analyzing word structure can reveal clues to its meaning, aiding comprehension.

Testing Your Answer Choice in Vocabulary Questions:

- By rereading the sentence with the answer choice in place of the vocabulary word, eliminate answers that don't make sense.
- By guessing the meaning of the word.
- By using a dictionary.
- By changing the sentence structure.

Correct Answer: By rereading the sentence with the answer choice in place of the vocabulary word, eliminate answers that don't make sense.

Explanation: This strategy ensures that chosen answers fit logically within the sentence, maintaining coherence.

Skimming Passages for Information:

- Avoid answering from memory; return to the passage to find and reread the relevant part before choosing your answer.

- Memorize the entire passage.

- Only focus on the first sentence.

- Ignore the details.

Correct Answer: Avoid answering from memory; return to the passage to find and reread the relevant part before choosing your answer.

Explanation: This technique enhances accuracy by confirming details directly from the text.

Using the Process of Elimination in Multiple Choice Tests:

- Eliminate answers you know are incorrect to improve your odds of selecting the right answer.

- Guess randomly.

- Choose the longest answer.

- Stick to the first choice.

Correct Answer: Eliminate answers you know are incorrect to improve your odds of selecting the right answer.

Explanation: Narrowing down choices increases the likelihood of identifying the correct answer.

Skipping Difficult Questions:

- If a question is challenging, circle it and move on. Return to it after answering others.

- Spend most of your time on it.

- Guess immediately.

- Ignore it completely.

Correct Answer: If a question is challenging, circle it and move on. Return to it after answering others.

Explanation: Revisiting difficult questions later can provide fresh perspective and increase accuracy.

Two Types of Vocabulary Questions:

- Synonyms/antonyms and complete the sentence.

- Sentence structure and grammar.

- Paragraph summaries and main ideas.

- Author's intent and tone.

Correct Answer: Synonyms/antonyms and complete the sentence.

Explanation: These question types test understanding of word meanings and contextual use.

Two Words Are Synonyms If:

- They have the same or nearly the same meaning.

- They have opposite meanings.

- They rhyme.

- They start with the same letter.

Correct Answer: They have the same or nearly the same meaning.

Explanation: Synonyms share similar meanings, enhancing vocabulary flexibility.

Antonyms Are:

- Two words with opposite meanings.

- Words that sound alike.

- Words with the same meaning.
- Words from the same root.

Correct Answer: Two words with opposite meanings.

Explanation: Antonyms provide contrast, enriching language comprehension.

Synonym and Antonym Questions Ask:

- For words with the same or opposite meaning as an underlined word in the question stem.
- For definitions.
- For example sentences.
- For rhyming words.

Correct Answer: For words with the same or opposite meaning as an underlined word in the question stem.

Explanation: These questions assess recognition of word relationships within contexts.

Most Common Mistake in Antonym Questions:

- Choosing a synonym instead of the antonym.
- Selecting the first choice.
- Guessing without reading.
- Choosing the longest word.

Correct Answer: Choosing a synonym instead of the antonym.

Explanation: This mistake reflects confusion between similar and opposite meanings.

Complete Sentence Questions Provide:

- A sentence with a single word missing; your job is to determine the best word from the choices.
- A list of synonyms.
- A paragraph summary.
- An author's opinion.

Correct Answer: A sentence with a single word missing; your job is to determine the best word from the choices.

Explanation: These questions test ability to use context to fill gaps in meaning.

To Answer a Complete the Sentence Question:

- Study the context of the missing word, using hints to determine its meaning.
- Guess based on first impressions.
- Choose the longest word.
- Ignore the context.

Correct Answer: Study the context of the missing word, using hints to determine its meaning.

Explanation: Contextual analysis aids in selecting words that logically complete sentences.

Spelling Questions Typically Provide:

- Three answer choices: one spelled correctly, two spelled incorrectly.
- Definitions for each word.
- Synonyms for each word.

- Antonyms for each word.

Correct Answer: Three answer choices: one spelled correctly, two spelled incorrectly.

Explanation: This format tests recognition of correct spelling amid common errors.

If Asked Which Is Not Spelled Correctly:

- The answer includes two correct spellings and one incorrect spelling.
- All options are incorrect.
- All options are correct.
- Only the first option is incorrect.

Correct Answer: The answer includes two correct spellings and one incorrect spelling.

Explanation: Identifying incorrect spelling requires discerning common misspellings.

Best Way to Review for Spelling Questions:

- Review spelling fundamentals and recognize when common rules are violated, but remember the exceptions in English.
- Memorize the dictionary.
- Focus only on long words.
- Ignore common words.

Correct Answer: Review spelling fundamentals and recognize when common rules are violated, but remember the exceptions in English.

Explanation: Familiarity with spelling rules and exceptions helps identify errors effectively.

I Before E Rule:

- Applies except after C, or when the word makes the long A sound (rhymes with way).
- Always true.
- Only for names.
- Never applies.

Correct Answer: Applies except after C, or when the word makes the long A sound (rhymes with way).

Explanation: This mnemonic aids in remembering a common spelling convention with notable exceptions.

GH Can Replace F or Be Silent:

- Examples include "enough" and "night."
- Only in short words.
- In every word.
- Never in English.

Correct Answer: Examples include "enough" and "night."

Explanation: The unique role of "gh" in English spelling can alter pronunciation, reflecting its complexity.

Adding an Ending to a Word That Ends in a Consonant:

- Double the consonant, as in "forget/forgettable" and "shop/shopping."
- Always remove the consonant.
- Never double the consonant.
- Only add vowels.

Correct Answer: Double the consonant, as in "forget/forgettable" and "shop/shopping."

Explanation: Doubling consonants when adding endings maintains correct pronunciation and spelling.

Adding a Suffix to a Word That Ends in E:

- Don't drop the E, as in "replace/replacement" and "peace/peaceful."
- Always drop the E.
- Only add consonants.
- Ignore the original word.

Correct Answer: Don't drop the E, as in "replace/replacement" and "peace/peaceful."

Explanation: Retaining the "E" in such cases preserves the word's integrity and meaning.

Dropping the E When Adding ING:

- Drop the E, as in "hope/hoping" and "dive/diving."
- Always keep the E.
- Only drop for short words.
- Ignore the rule entirely.

Correct Answer: Drop the E, as in "hope/hoping" and "dive/diving."

Explanation: Removing the "E" before adding "ing" ensures proper grammatical form.

Spelling of Prefixes and Suffixes:

- Generally remains unchanged, e.g., project, propel, proactive.
- Always changes.
- Only changes if the word is long.
- Changes with every word.

Correct Answer: Generally remains unchanged, e.g., project, propel, proactive.

Explanation: Prefixes and suffixes typically maintain their spelling, preserving the root's structure and meaning.

Plural of Words Ending in a Consonant and Y:

- Change the Y to I and add ES, e.g., baby/babies, filly/fillies.
- Just add S.
- Add only ES.
- Remove the Y completely.

Correct Answer: Change the Y to I and add ES, e.g., baby/babies, filly/fillies.

Explanation: This rule ensures correct pluralization for words ending in a consonant and Y.

Plural of Words Ending in a Vowel and Y:

- Just add S, e.g., monkey/monkeys, day/days.
- Change the Y to I.
- Add ES.
- Remove the Y.

Correct Answer: Just add S, e.g., monkey/monkeys, day/days.

Explanation: The presence of a vowel before Y simplifies pluralization to merely adding S.

Prefix "ama/amo":

- Means love, e.g., amateur, amorous.
- Means hate.
- Means fear.
- Means confusion.

Correct Answer: Means love, e.g., amateur, amorous.

Explanation: This prefix relates to affection or fondness, as shown in derived words.

Prefix "ambi":

- Means both, e.g., ambivalent, ambidextrous.
- Means one.
- Means none.
- Means above.

Correct Answer: Means both, e.g., ambivalent, ambidextrous.

Explanation: The prefix "ambi" indicates duality or simultaneous presence.

Prefix "aud":

- Means hear, e.g., audition, audible.
- Means see.
- Means touch.
- Means smell.

Correct Answer: Means hear, e.g., audition, audible.

Explanation: This prefix is related to sound and listening, reflecting auditory concepts.

Prefix "bell":

- Means war, e.g., belligerent, bellicose.
- Means peace.
- Means love.
- Means flight.

Correct Answer: Means war, e.g., belligerent, bellicose.

Explanation: Terms derived from "bell" often denote conflict or aggression.

Prefix "bene":

- Means good, e.g., benefactor, benediction.
- Means bad.
- Means average.
- Means neutral.

Correct Answer: Means good, e.g., benefactor, benediction.

Explanation: This prefix associates with beneficial or positive actions and qualities.

Prefix "cid/cis":

- Means cut, e.g., homicide, scissors.
- Means join.
- Means build.
- Means cover.

Correct Answer: Means cut, e.g., homicide, scissors.

Explanation: "Cid/cis" implies division or separation, often in a decisive manner.

Prefix "cogn/gno":

- Means know, e.g., cognitive, recognize.
- Means forget.
- Means ignore.
- Means hide.

Correct Answer: Means know, e.g., cognitive, recognize.

Explanation: This prefix relates to knowledge and awareness, emphasizing understanding.

Prefix "curr":

- Means run, e.g., current.
- Means stop.
- Means slow.
- Means stand.

Correct Answer: Means run, e.g., current.

Explanation: "Curr" pertains to movement or flow, often in a forward direction.

Prefix "flu/flux":

- Means flow, e.g., fluid, fluctuate.
- Means standstill.
- Means block.
- Means freeze.

Correct Answer: Means flow, e.g., fluid, fluctuate.

Explanation: This prefix signifies movement or change, typically in a smooth manner.

Prefix "gress":

- Means to go, e.g., congress, congregation.
- Means to stop.
- Means to rest.
- Means to retreat.

Correct Answer: Means to go, e.g., congress, congregation.

Explanation: "Gress" indicates progress or movement, often towards a goal or together.

Prefix "in":

- Means not, in, e.g., ingenious, integral.

- Means out.
- Means over.
- Means under.

Correct Answer: Means not, in, e.g., ingenious, integral.

Explanation: This prefix can either negate or incorporate, affecting meaning significantly.

Prefix "ject":

- Means throw, e.g., inject, reject.
- Means catch.
- Means hold.
- Means place.

Correct Answer: Means throw, e.g., inject, reject.

Explanation: "Ject" involves propulsion or forceful movement, often altering position.

Prefix "luc/lux":

- Means light, e.g., lucid, translucent.
- Means dark.
- Means heavy.
- Means thick.

Correct Answer: Means light, e.g., lucid, translucent.

Explanation: This prefix relates to illumination or clarity, enhancing visibility or understanding.

Prefix "neo":

- Means new, e.g., neophyte, neoconservative.
- Means old.
- Means ancient.
- Means distant.

Correct Answer: Means new, e.g., neophyte, neoconservative.

Explanation: "Neo" signifies recent or modern, indicating novelty or innovation.

Prefix "omni":

- Means all, e.g., omnivorous, omnipotent.
- Means none.
- Means some.
- Means few.

Correct Answer: Means all, e.g., omnivorous, omnipotent.

Explanation: This prefix conveys totality or universality, reflecting completeness.

Prefix "pel/puls":

- Means push, e.g., impulse, propeller.
- Means pull.
- Means hold.

63

- Means stop.

Correct Answer: Means push, e.g., impulse, propeller.

Explanation: "Pel/puls" involves exerting force or motion, often driving forward.

Prefix "pro":

- Means forward, e.g., project, produce.

- Means backward.

- Means sideways.

- Means still.

Correct Answer: Means forward, e.g., project, produce.

Explanation: "Pro" suggests advancement or enhancement, indicating progress.

Prefix "psuedo":

- Means false, e.g., pseudonym, pseudoscientific.

- Means true.

- Means sure.

- Means real.

Correct Answer: Means false, e.g., pseudonym, pseudoscientific.

Explanation: This prefix denotes imitation or deceit, often signifying a facade.

Prefix "rog":

- Means ask, e.g., interrogate.

- Means answer.

- Means ignore.

- Means hide.

Correct Answer: Means ask, e.g., interrogate.

Explanation: "Rog" involves inquiry or questioning, emphasizing information-seeking.

Prefix "sub":

- Means under, e.g., subjugate, subterranean.

- Means over.

- Means above.

- Means next to.

Correct Answer: Means under, e.g., subjugate, subterranean.

Explanation: This prefix indicates a position beneath or supporting, often suggesting hierarchy or depth.

Prefix "spec/spic":

- Means look, see, e.g., spectator, spectacles.

- Means hear.

- Means touch.

- Means taste.

Correct Answer: Means look, see, e.g., spectator, spectacles.

Explanation: These prefixes pertain to vision or observation, enhancing visual understanding.

Prefix "super":

- Means over, e.g., superfluous, supercede.
- Means under.
- Means beneath.
- Means beside.

Correct Answer: Means over, e.g., superfluous, supercede.

Explanation: "Super" conveys excess or superiority, often implying dominance or abundance.

Prefix "temp":

- Means time, e.g., contemporary, temporal.
- Means space.
- Means distance.
- Means place.

Correct Answer: Means time, e.g., contemporary, temporal.

Explanation: This prefix relates to duration or chronology, influencing temporal context.

Prefix "un":

- Means not, opposite, e.g., uncoordinated, uninvited.
- Means similar.
- Means same.
- Means together.

Correct Answer: Means not, opposite, e.g., uncoordinated, uninvited.

Explanation: "Un" negates or reverses, altering meaning to depict absence or contradiction.

Prefix "viv":

- Means live, e.g., vivid, vivacious.
- Means die.
- Means dull.
- Means slow.

Correct Answer: Means live, e.g., vivid, vivacious.

Explanation: This prefix emphasizes life, energy, and vibrancy in its meanings.

Grammar Questions Typically Present:

- Three variations of a sentence, asking which is correct. Incorrect answers contain identifiable errors.
- Only one correct answer.
- Two correct answers.
- No correct answers.

Correct Answer: Three variations of a sentence, asking which is correct. Incorrect answers contain identifiable errors.

Explanation: This format evaluates understanding of grammar by presenting alternatives with common errors.

Incomplete Sentences Are Called:

- Sentence fragments.

- Complete sentences.

- Paragraphs.

- Essays.

Correct Answer: Sentence fragments.

Explanation: Fragments lack completeness, failing to express a full thought.

A Complete Sentence Expresses:

- A complete, independent thought. If words can stand alone with understandable meaning, they form a sentence.

- A partial idea.

- A complex thesis.

- A list of words.

Correct Answer: A complete, independent thought. If words can stand alone with understandable meaning, they form a sentence.

Explanation: Complete sentences convey full ideas, essential for clear communication.

Distinguishing Sentences from Fragments:

- Be mindful of answer choices starting with subordinating conjunctions, as these often indicate sentence fragments.

- Ignore the conjunctions.

- Focus only on the verbs.

- Concentrate on the nouns.

Correct Answer: Be mindful of answer choices starting with subordinating conjunctions, as these often indicate sentence fragments.

Explanation: Subordinating conjunctions often introduce dependent clauses, which need additional information to form complete sentences.

List of Subordinating Conjunctions:

- Includes words like after, although, because, and while.

- Contains verbs.

- Lists proper nouns.

- Consists of adjectives.

Correct Answer: Includes words like after, although, because, and while.

Explanation: These conjunctions connect dependent clauses to independent ones, indicating additional context is needed.

Answer Choices Starting with Subordinating Conjunctions:

- Often form sentence fragments needing more information to complete the thought.

- Are always complete sentences.

- Never require additional context.

- Are always grammatically correct.

Correct Answer: Often form sentence fragments needing more information to complete the thought.

Explanation: These words suggest that the clause is incomplete without further context or a main clause.

Run-On Sentence Contains:

- More than one independent clause not properly connected.
- Only one clause.
- No verbs.
- No subjects.

Correct Answer: More than one independent clause not properly connected.

Explanation: Run-on sentences lack proper punctuation or conjunctions to separate independent clauses, leading to confusion.

Connecting Two Independent Clauses Properly:

- Use a conjunction or appropriate punctuation like a semi-colon or colon.
- Use no punctuation.
- Use only commas.
- Avoid conjunctions.

Correct Answer: Use a conjunction or appropriate punctuation like a semi-colon or colon.

Explanation: Proper connection prevents run-on sentences, ensuring clarity and grammatical correctness.

Turning One of the Independent Clauses Into a Prepositional Phrase:

- Use a preposition.
- Use a conjunction.
- Add a verb.
- Remove all punctuation.

Correct Answer: Use a preposition.

Explanation: A preposition can transform an independent clause into a dependent phrase, altering sentence structure.

Determining a Complete and Correct Sentence:

- Ensure it has both a subject and a verb, and is not a run-on.
- Ignore the subject.
- Use only verbs.
- Avoid punctuation.

Correct Answer: Ensure it has both a subject and a verb, and is not a run-on.

Explanation: A complete sentence requires both elements to convey a full thought, avoiding grammatical errors.

Most Common Capitalization Rules:

- Capitalize the first word in a sentence, complete quotations, proper nouns, and proper adjectives.
- Never capitalize proper nouns.
- Ignore sentence beginnings.

- Capitalize only verbs.

Correct Answer: Capitalize the first word in a sentence, complete quotations, proper nouns, and proper adjectives.

Explanation: Proper capitalization enhances readability and respects grammatical conventions.

Days of the Week and Months of the Year:
- Should be capitalized, e.g., Friday, January.
- Never capitalized.
- Always lowercase.
- Capitalized only in titles.

Correct Answer: Should be capitalized, e.g., Friday, January.

Explanation: These are proper nouns, representing specific periods, requiring capitalization.

Holidays and Special Events:
- Should be capitalized, e.g., Christmas, Halloween.
- Always lowercase.
- Never capitalized.
- Only capitalized in formal writing.

Correct Answer: Should be capitalized, e.g., Christmas, Halloween.

Explanation: As proper nouns, holidays signify unique occasions, necessitating capitalization.

Names of Individuals:
- Should be capitalized, e.g., John Henry.
- Always lowercase.
- Never capitalized.
- Capitalized only in signatures.

Correct Answer: Should be capitalized, e.g., John Henry.

Explanation: Capitalizing names shows respect and identifies individuals properly.

Names of Structures and Buildings:
- Should be capitalized, e.g., Lincoln Memorial.
- Always lowercase.
- Only capitalized in blueprints.
- Never capitalized.

Correct Answer: Should be capitalized, e.g., Lincoln Memorial.

Explanation: These are specific titles of places, requiring capitalization for proper identification.

Names of Trains, Ships, Aircraft:
- Should be capitalized, e.g., Queen Elizabeth.
- Always lowercase.
- Only capitalized in logs.
- Never capitalized.

Correct Answer: Should be capitalized, e.g., Queen Elizabeth.

Explanation: Proper nouns, like names of vehicles, are capitalized to denote specific entities.

Product Names:

- Should be capitalized, e.g., Corn King hams.
- Always lowercase.
- Never capitalized.
- Capitalized only in ads.

Correct Answer: Should be capitalized, e.g., Corn King hams.

Explanation: Capitalizing product names distinguishes them as specific brands or items.

Cities and States:

- Should be capitalized, e.g., Des Moines, Iowa.
- Always lowercase.
- Never capitalized.
- Only capitalized on maps.

Correct Answer: Should be capitalized, e.g., Des Moines, Iowa.

Explanation: These are proper nouns, representing unique geographical locations, requiring capitalization.

Streets, Highways, and Roads:

- Should be capitalized, e.g., Grand Avenue.
- Always lowercase.
- Never capitalized.
- Only capitalized in maps.

Correct Answer: Should be capitalized, e.g., Grand Avenue.

Explanation: Capitalization of street names indicates specific places, aiding in navigation and reference.

Landmarks and Public Areas:

- Should be capitalized, e.g., Grand Canyon.
- Always lowercase.
- Never capitalized.
- Only capitalized in brochures.

Correct Answer: Should be capitalized, e.g., Grand Canyon.

Explanation: These are unique sites, and their capitalization acknowledges their significance.

Bodies of Water:

- Should be capitalized, e.g., Atlantic Ocean.
- Always lowercase.
- Never capitalized.
- Only capitalized in atlases.

Correct Answer: Should be capitalized, e.g., Atlantic Ocean.

Explanation: Proper nouns, such as water bodies, are capitalized to specify their uniqueness.

Ethnic Groups, Languages, Nationalities:

- Should be capitalized, e.g., Asian American.

- Always lowercase.

- Never capitalized.

- Only capitalized in official documents.

Correct Answer: Should be capitalized, e.g., Asian American.

Explanation: Capitalizing these terms shows respect and acknowledges cultural identity.

Official Titles:

- Should be capitalized, e.g., Mayor Daley.

- Always lowercase.

- Never capitalized.

- Only capitalized in announcements.

Correct Answer: Should be capitalized, e.g., Mayor Daley.

Explanation: Capitalizing titles highlights authority and distinguishes positions.

Institutions, Organizations, Businesses:

- Should be capitalized, e.g., Dartmouth College.

- Always lowercase.

- Never capitalized.

- Only capitalized in contracts.

Correct Answer: Should be capitalized, e.g., Dartmouth College.

Explanation: These names are proper nouns, recognized for their distinct identity and importance.

Proper Adjectives:

- Should be capitalized, e.g., English muffin.

- Always lowercase.

- Never capitalized.

- Only capitalized in recipes.

Correct Answer: Should be capitalized, e.g., English muffin.

Explanation: Proper adjectives derive from proper nouns, maintaining capitalization to reflect origin.

When to Use a Period:

- At the end of statements, after initials, and abbreviations (unless an acronym).

- Only with questions.

- Never with abbreviations.

- Only in titles.

Correct Answer: At the end of statements, after initials, and abbreviations (unless an acronym).

Explanation: Periods signal sentence completion and clarify abbreviations, ensuring concise communication.

Most Common Uses of a Comma:

- Use a comma before coordinating conjunctions like and, but, or when separating independent clauses; to separate items in a list; with multiple adjectives for the same noun; after introductory elements; in names with Jr., Sr.; in addresses; between a day and year; after greetings and closings in letters; with contrasting elements; to set off appositives.

- Never use commas.

- Only use commas with numbers.

- Use commas only in poetry.

Correct Answer: Use a comma before coordinating conjunctions like and, but, or when separating independent clauses; to separate items in a list; with multiple adjectives for the same noun; after introductory elements; in names with Jr., Sr.; in addresses; between a day and year; after greetings and closings in letters; with contrasting elements; to set off appositives.

Explanation: Commas clarify meaning and structure in sentences, enhancing readability and preventing confusion.

Full-Length Practice Test 1 (170 Q&A and Explanations)

Main Rules for Using Apostrophes:

- Show letters omitted in contractions and indicate possession.

- Never use apostrophes.

- Use only for plurals.

- Always place at the end of sentences.

Correct Answer: Show letters omitted in contractions and indicate possession.

Explanation: Apostrophes indicate missing letters in contractions or ownership, essential for clarity in writing.

Rules for Using Quotations:

- Complete sentence quotes start with a capital letter and a preceding comma, with punctuation inside. Non-complete sentence quotes start lower case, with end punctuation only if at the sentence's end. Use single quotations inside double ones.

- Never use punctuation with quotes.

- Always use double quotes.

- Quotes never need commas.

Correct Answer: Complete sentence quotes start with a capital letter and a preceding comma, with punctuation inside. Non-complete sentence quotes start lower case, with end punctuation only if at the sentence's end. Use single quotations inside double ones.

Explanation: Proper quotation formatting ensures clarity and distinguishes quoted material from the surrounding text.

Subject and Verb Agreement:

- Subjects and verbs must agree in number; singular subjects with singular verbs, plural with plural.

- Always use plural verbs.

- Ignore the subject.

- Use any verb form.

Correct Answer: Subjects and verbs must agree in number; singular subjects with singular verbs, plural with plural.

Explanation: Agreement ensures grammatical accuracy, aiding reader comprehension and sentence coherence.

Pronoun Subjects:

- Some pronouns are always singular, others plural, while some can be either, depending on context.
- Always singular.
- Always plural.
- Never change.

Correct Answer: Some pronouns are always singular, others plural, while some can be either, depending on context.

Explanation: Proper pronoun usage maintains grammatical consistency and prevents ambiguity.

Always Singular Pronouns:

- Include words like anybody, anyone, each, either, everyone, neither, nobody, one, someone.
- Always plural.
- Always change.
- Never singular.

Correct Answer: Include words like anybody, anyone, each, either, everyone, neither, nobody, one, someone.

Explanation: These pronouns inherently refer to individual entities, requiring singular verbs.

Avoiding Mismatched Pronouns:

- Add "one" mentally after each, either, neither to ensure singular agreement.
- Always use plural verbs.
- Never change pronouns.
- Ignore verb form.

Correct Answer: Add "one" mentally after each, either, neither to ensure singular agreement.

Explanation: This mental check helps maintain subject-verb agreement, avoiding common errors.

Always Plural Pronouns:

- Include both, few, many, several.
- Always singular.
- Never change.
- Always neutral.

Correct Answer: Include both, few, many, several.

Explanation: These pronouns inherently refer to multiple entities, necessitating plural verbs.

Pronouns That Can Be Singular or Plural:

- Depend on following words or phrases for verb agreement; include all, any, most, none, some.
- Always singular.
- Always plural.
- Never change.

Correct Answer: Depend on following words or phrases for verb agreement; include all, any, most, none, some.

Explanation: Context determines whether these pronouns take singular or plural verbs, requiring careful analysis.

Subjects Joined by "And":

- Form compound subjects, taking plural verbs.
- Always singular.
- Never change.
- Always singular verbs.

Correct Answer: Form compound subjects, taking plural verbs.

Explanation: Compound subjects imply multiple entities, thus requiring plural verb forms.

Subjects Joined by "Or" or "Nor":

- Agree with the noun or pronoun closest to the verb.
- Always plural.
- Always singular.
- Never change.

Correct Answer: Agree with the noun or pronoun closest to the verb.

Explanation: The proximity rule ensures correct subject-verb agreement, preventing grammatical errors.

Present Tense Verbs:

- Indicate actions happening currently.
- Always past.
- Always future.
- Never change.

Correct Answer: Indicate actions happening currently.

Explanation: Present tense conveys immediacy or ongoing action, essential for real-time context.

Past Tense Verbs:

- Indicate actions already completed.
- Always present.
- Always future.
- Never change.

Correct Answer: Indicate actions already completed.

Explanation: Past tense provides historical context, indicating actions that have occurred.

Future Tense Verbs:

- Indicate actions yet to happen.
- Always past.
- Always present.
- Never change.

Correct Answer: Indicate actions yet to happen.

Explanation: Future tense signals forthcoming actions, preparing readers for subsequent events.

Pronouns Replacing Other Pronouns:

- Must agree in number.
- Always singular.
- Always plural.
- Never change.

Correct Answer: Must agree in number.

Explanation: Consistent agreement prevents confusion, ensuring clarity and grammatical accuracy.

Pronouns Joined by "And":

- Use a plural pronoun to represent them.
- Always singular.
- Always plural.
- Never change.

Correct Answer: Use a plural pronoun to represent them.

Explanation: "And" suggests multiple entities, necessitating plural pronouns.

Singular Nouns/Pronouns Joined by "Or" or "Nor":

- Use a singular pronoun to represent them.
- Always plural.
- Always singular.
- Never change.

Correct Answer: Use a singular pronoun to represent them.

Explanation: Singular nouns joined by "or" or "nor" imply one choice, requiring singular pronouns.

Singular and Plural Nouns/Pronouns Joined by "Or" or "Nor":

- Choose the pronoun agreeing with the one after "or" or "nor."
- Always singular.
- Always plural.
- Never change.

Correct Answer: Choose the pronoun agreeing with the one after "or" or "nor."

Explanation: This ensures subject-verb agreement, aligning with the nearest noun or pronoun.

Active Voice:

- The subject performs the action.
- Always passive.
- Never changes.
- Always indirect.

Correct Answer: The subject performs the action.

Explanation: Active voice emphasizes the subject's role, providing clarity and directness.

Passive Voice:

- The subject receives the action.
- Always active.
- Never changes.
- Always indirect.

Correct Answer: The subject receives the action.

Explanation: Passive voice shifts focus from the subject to the action, often used for stylistic reasons.

Preferred Voice:

- Active voice is usually preferred; passive is occasionally correct but often less effective.
- Always passive.
- Never active.
- Always indirect.

Correct Answer: Active voice is usually preferred; passive is occasionally correct but often less effective.

Explanation: Active voice enhances clarity and engagement, while passive voice may obscure the subject.

Modifier:

- A descriptive word, phrase, or clause that should be clearly linked to what it describes.
- Always a noun.
- Never changes.
- Always indirect.

Correct Answer: A descriptive word, phrase, or clause that should be clearly linked to what it describes.

Explanation: Properly placed modifiers ensure clear communication, avoiding ambiguity and confusion.

Dangling Modifier:

- Refers to an unstated concept, creating confusion.
- Always clear.
- Never changes.
- Always direct.

Correct Answer: Refers to an unstated concept, creating confusion.

Explanation: Dangling modifiers obscure meaning, requiring revision for clarity and precision.

Redundant Sentence:

- Repeats ideas unnecessarily.
- Always concise.
- Never changes.
- Always direct.

Correct Answer: Repeats ideas unnecessarily.

Explanation: Redundancy clutters writing, reducing efficiency and clarity, thus should be avoided.

Wordy Sentence:

- Contains unnecessary words, best expressed more concisely.

- Always concise.

- Never changes.

- Always indirect.

Correct Answer: Contains unnecessary words, best expressed more concisely.

Explanation: Conciseness improves readability and engagement, eliminating superfluous language.

Mean:

- The average, calculated by adding all numbers and dividing by their count.

- Always the highest.

- Always the lowest.

- Never changes.

Correct Answer: The average, calculated by adding all numbers and dividing by their count.

Explanation: Calculating the mean provides a central value, summarizing data sets effectively.

Median:

- The middle number in a lined-up sequence.

- Always the highest.

- Always the lowest.

- Never changes.

Correct Answer: The middle number in a lined-up sequence.

Explanation: The median centralizes data, offering a midpoint unaffected by extreme values.

Mode:

- The number that appears most frequently.

- Always the highest.

- Always the lowest.

- Never changes.

Correct Answer: The number that appears most frequently.

Explanation: Mode identifies the most common value, highlighting trends or patterns in data.

Range:

- The difference between the highest and lowest numbers.

- Always the highest.

- Always the lowest.

- Never changes.

Correct Answer: The difference between the highest and lowest numbers.

Explanation: Range provides insight into data variability or spread, indicating distribution breadth.

Definition of Authority:

- The power or right to give commands, enforce obedience, take action, and make decisions.

- The ability to speak loudly.

- The right to wear a uniform.

- The capacity to write reports.

Correct Answer: The power or right to give commands, enforce obedience, take action, and make decisions.

Explanation: Authority is the legitimate power vested in a ranger to maintain order and ensure compliance with park regulations and laws.

Primary Objective of Park Ranger's Enforcement Actions:

- Education and information.

- Issuing fines.

- Arresting offenders.

- Ignoring minor infractions.

Correct Answer: Education and information.

Explanation: The goal is to help visitors understand rules and the importance of park preservation, promoting voluntary compliance.

Least Likely Ranger Service Through Visitor Contact:

- Resource management.

- Giving directions.

- Providing safety advice.

- Explaining park features.

Correct Answer: Resource management.

Explanation: Resource management typically involves behind-the-scenes work on conservation and ecological balance, separate from direct visitor interaction.

First Action at a Crime Scene Without Investigation Training:

- Record existing and relevant data in a notebook.

- Attempt to investigate.

- Leave the scene immediately.

- Arrest anyone nearby.

Correct Answer: Record existing and relevant data in a notebook.

Explanation: Documenting details ensures crucial evidence is preserved for trained investigators to handle further.

Location of VIN Plate in Most Automobiles:

- The driver's dashboard.

- Under the hood.

- In the trunk.

- On the passenger door.

Correct Answer: The driver's dashboard.

Explanation: The VIN (Vehicle Identification Number) is typically located on the dashboard near the windshield, visible from outside.

Surface for a Park's Situation Map:

- Enamel or clear acetate.

- Wood.

- Fabric.

- Metal.

Correct Answer: Enamel or clear acetate.

Explanation: These materials allow for easy updates and durability, important for accurate and reliable information display.

Rhomberg Test Usefulness:

- Alcohol intoxication.

- Drug identification.

- Physical fitness.

- Vision testing.

Correct Answer: Alcohol intoxication.

Explanation: The Rhomberg test assesses an individual's balance and coordination, often impaired by alcohol consumption.

Key Responsibility for a Ranger on Patrol:

- Observation.

- Writing reports.

- Engaging in conversation.

- Distributing flyers.

Correct Answer: Observation.

Explanation: Observing surroundings ensures safety, detects potential issues, and allows for quick response to incidents.

Rare Form of Federal Jurisdiction Encountered by Rangers:

- Partial jurisdiction.

- Full jurisdiction.

- Concurrent jurisdiction.

- Exclusive jurisdiction.

Correct Answer: Partial jurisdiction.

Explanation: Partial jurisdiction involves limited federal authority, seldom encountered, as it requires specific agreements with states.

Key to Issuing a Verbal Warning:

- Maintain a stern and authoritative tone of voice.

- Speak softly.

- Use complicated language.

- Avoid eye contact.

Correct Answer: Maintain a stern and authoritative tone of voice.

Explanation: A clear, firm tone conveys seriousness, encouraging compliance without escalating the situation.

Most Appropriate Training Vehicle for Rangers with Law Enforcement Authority:

- Orientation course, on-the-job training, and special training courses.
- Online classes only.
- Monthly seminars.
- Independent study.

Correct Answer: Orientation course, on-the-job training, and special training courses.

Explanation: Comprehensive training ensures rangers are well-prepared for diverse law enforcement scenarios.

Use of Vehicles for Park Patrol:

- Increases response speed, offers protection, and is efficient with limited manpower.
- Reduces visibility.
- Increases noise pollution.
- Limits ranger interaction.

Correct Answer: Increases response speed, offers protection, and is efficient with limited manpower.

Explanation: Vehicles enhance mobility and safety, enabling rangers to cover more ground and respond swiftly.

Standard Kneeling Search Procedure:

- Search behind the offender.
- Search in front.
- Search from the side.
- Avoid contact.

Correct Answer: Search behind the offender.

Explanation: This position offers control and safety, minimizing risk to the ranger during the search process.

Immediate Responsibility in Enforcement Communication:

- Create a supportive rather than a defensive climate.
- Demand immediate compliance.
- Ignore visitor concerns.
- Use aggressive language.

Correct Answer: Create a supportive rather than a defensive climate.

Explanation: A supportive approach encourages cooperation and reduces tension, facilitating effective communication.

Knot Used to Attach a Rope to the Middle of Another Rope:

- Prusik.
- Bowline.
- Square knot.
- Clove hitch.

Correct Answer: Prusik.

Explanation: The Prusik knot is a type of friction hitch that allows for secure connection and easy adjustment along the rope.

Highest Level of Listening:

- Listening with understanding of the speaker's point of view.
- Hearing only key words.
- Focusing on your response.
- Ignoring non-verbal cues.

Correct Answer: Listening with understanding of the speaker's point of view.

Explanation: This level of listening fosters empathy and effective communication by fully grasping the speaker's perspective.

Structures Entered Unconditionally by Rangers:

- Park administrative building and public restrooms.
- Private residences.
- Visitor's tents.
- Unmarked storage facilities.

Correct Answer: Park administrative building and public restrooms.

Explanation: These areas are public spaces within a ranger's jurisdiction, allowing for unrestricted access during enforcement.

Standard Item for Mounted Patrol:

- Flares.
- First aid kit.
- Water bottle.
- Binoculars.

Correct Answer: Flares.

Explanation: Flares are essential for signaling and safety purposes, especially in low-visibility conditions, making them a standard item for mounted patrol.

"Thumbnail" Descriptions of Persons Include:

- Hair color, clothing, and race.
- Height and weight only.
- Eye color and age only.
- Footwear and accessories only.

Correct Answer: Hair color, clothing, and race.

Explanation: "Thumbnail" descriptions provide quick, essential identifiers that help in recognizing or locating individuals effectively.

Grid Map Reference Number Location:

- Right and above the point of intersection of the lines relating to the grid numbers.
- Left and below.
- Directly on the point.

- In the center of the grid.

Correct Answer: Right and above the point of intersection of the lines relating to the grid numbers.

Explanation: This convention ensures consistent navigation and communication when using grid maps for location identification.

Permissible Search During Arrest:

- During a legal search, a ranger may seize items that are not only in actual possession, but within reach of the person at the time of the search.
- Only items in pockets.
- Items must be in sight.
- Search is not allowed.

Correct Answer: During a legal search, a ranger may seize items that are not only in actual possession, but within reach of the person at the time of the search.

Explanation: This rule ensures safety and prevents the destruction of evidence during an arrest.

Best Text-on-Background Color for Legibility:

- Blue on white.
- Red on black.
- Yellow on green.
- Black on purple.

Correct Answer: Blue on white.

Explanation: This combination offers high contrast and readability, crucial for visitor comprehension at exhibits.

Search Warrant Requirement:

- The search is of a habitable dwelling on park grounds that is owned by the park, but occupied by the suspect as a camping abode.
- For any vehicle.
- For open areas.
- For public restrooms.

Correct Answer: The search is of a habitable dwelling on park grounds that is owned by the park, but occupied by the suspect as a camping abode.

Explanation: Legal protection for dwellings mandates a warrant to respect privacy and lawful procedure.

Primary Objective of Interpretive Services:

- Inciting the visitor to some action or feeling.
- Selling souvenirs.
- Collecting entrance fees.
- Limiting visitor questions.

Correct Answer: Inciting the visitor to some action or feeling.

Explanation: Interpretive services aim to engage and inspire visitors, enhancing their appreciation and understanding of the park.

Consent Searches:

- Consent may be revoked at any time, but the revocation does not invalidate any evidence seized prior to the revocation.

- Consent is permanent.

- Evidence must be returned if consent is revoked.

- Consent must be written.

Correct Answer: Consent may be revoked at any time, but the revocation does not invalidate any evidence seized prior to the revocation.

Explanation: Consent searches balance personal rights with law enforcement needs, ensuring legal adherence.

Visitor Perception by Rangers:

- Not dependent on the ranger; it is the ranger who is dependent on them, the most important people the ranger will come into contact with, not an interruption of the ranger's work, but the main reason for it.

- Annoyances to be managed.

- Secondary to park duties.

- Primarily rule-breakers.

Correct Answer: Not dependent on the ranger; it is the ranger who is dependent on them, the most important people the ranger will come into contact with, not an interruption of the ranger's work, but the main reason for it.

Explanation: Visitors are the focus of park services, and their experience is central to a ranger's role.

Legal Term Denoting Proof of Crime:

- Corpus Delicti.

- Habeas Corpus.

- Prima Facie.

- Res Ipsa Loquitur.

Correct Answer: Corpus Delicti.

Explanation: This term refers to the objective proof that a crime has occurred, necessary for legal proceedings.

Priority 1 Situations in Enforcement:

- Protection of visitors from each other.

- Maintenance of park facilities.

- Wildlife preservation.

- Issuing parking tickets.

Correct Answer: Protection of visitors from each other.

Explanation: Ensuring visitor safety is paramount, requiring immediate attention to prevent harm.

Strongest Rope Material:

- Nylon.

- Cotton.

- Hemp.

- Polyester.

Correct Answer: Nylon.

Explanation: Nylon is known for its strength and durability, making it ideal for rigorous applications.

Text Size for Exhibits Viewed from 15 Feet:

- At least an inch high.
- Half an inch.
- Two inches.
- A quarter inch.

Correct Answer: At least an inch high.

Explanation: Appropriate text size ensures readability from a distance, enhancing visitor engagement with exhibits.

Primary Purposes of Patrol:

- Providing resource protection, making assistance available to visitors, providing a deterrent for destructive behavior, observing the park and visitor behavior.
- Selling tickets.
- Collecting litter.
- Conducting surveys.

Correct Answer: Providing resource protection, making assistance available to visitors, providing a deterrent for destructive behavior, observing the park and visitor behavior.

Explanation: Patrols serve multiple functions, ensuring both the safety and enjoyment of visitors and the preservation of park resources.

Preliminary Procedures for Crime Scene:

- Safeguarding the area, separating witnesses from bystanders and obtaining statements, rendering assistance to the injured.
- Arrest all present.
- Ignore witnesses.
- Focus only on evidence collection.

Correct Answer: Safeguarding the area, separating witnesses from bystanders and obtaining statements, rendering assistance to the injured.

Explanation: These actions preserve evidence integrity and support investigation while ensuring safety and assistance.

Jurisdiction Type with Only State Law in Effect:

- Proprietary jurisdiction.
- Concurrent jurisdiction.
- Exclusive jurisdiction.
- Full jurisdiction.

Correct Answer: Proprietary jurisdiction.

Explanation: This jurisdiction limits federal enforcement, relying primarily on state law, except where federal laws specifically apply.

Legal Requirements for a Search Warrant:

- Property to be seized, place to be searched, limits of the search, probable cause upon which the search is based.
- Only the suspect's name.
- The ranger's badge number.
- The time of day.

Correct Answer: Property to be seized, place to be searched, limits of the search, probable cause upon which the search is based.

Explanation: Specificity in a search warrant protects individual rights and ensures legal compliance.

Guideline for Handling Domestic Disputes:

- If the situation seems to justify the intervention of a professional counselor, recommend counseling in a general way.
- Immediately arrest both parties.
- Ignore the situation.
- Advise separation without further action.

Correct Answer: If the situation seems to justify the intervention of a professional counselor, recommend counseling in a general way.

Explanation: Offering guidance towards counseling supports resolution and safety without imposing direct intervention.

Communication with Subcultures:

- Understand the "language" of subculture, but not to use it.
- Mimic their language.
- Ignore their language.
- Use formal language only.

Correct Answer: Understand the "language" of subculture, but not to use it.

Explanation: Understanding aids effective communication, while maintaining professionalism ensures respect and authority.

Empowerment of Rangers Without Law Enforcement Authority:

- Issue citations in some situations.
- Arrest suspects.
- Conduct full searches.
- Confiscate personal items.

Correct Answer: Issue citations in some situations.

Explanation: Even without full law enforcement authority, rangers can still enforce certain regulations by issuing citations, maintaining order and compliance.

Disadvantage of Foot Patrol:

- Limited ability to respond to situations outside the immediate area.
- High visibility.
- Increased interaction with visitors.

- Enhanced observation opportunities.

Correct Answer: Limited ability to respond to situations outside the immediate area.

Explanation: Being on foot restricts a ranger's mobility, making it challenging to quickly reach incidents occurring at a distance.

Guidelines for Search-and-Rescue Operations:

- Radio-equipped searchers to vantage points, dogs on leashes, no night searches unless life-threatening, searchers call out names.
- Use only helicopters.
- Search only during daylight.
- Allow dogs to roam freely.

Correct Answer: Radio-equipped searchers to vantage points, dogs on leashes, no night searches unless life-threatening, searchers call out names.

Explanation: These guidelines ensure effective, safe, and organized search efforts while minimizing risks to both searchers and the lost individuals.

Least Likely Factor Affecting Enforcement Services:

- The ranger's level of certainty about the appropriateness of enforcement.
- Availability of resources.
- Legal authority and jurisdiction.
- Training and experience.

Correct Answer: The ranger's level of certainty about the appropriateness of enforcement.

Explanation: Enforcement decisions are typically guided by established protocols and laws, rather than personal certainty, ensuring consistency and legality.

Good Listening Skills:

- Considering listening to be an active process.
- Interrupting frequently.
- Focusing on your own response.
- Avoiding eye contact.

Correct Answer: Considering listening to be an active process.

Explanation: Active listening involves full engagement with the speaker, facilitating effective communication and understanding.

Not Part of Standard Frisk Procedures:

- Ranger moves fingertips over all searchable areas, crushing clothing to locate concealed weapons.
- Checking pockets.
- Patting down outer clothing.
- Removing hats.

Correct Answer: Ranger moves fingertips over all searchable areas, crushing clothing to locate concealed weapons.

Explanation: Standard frisk procedures involve a careful pat-down to detect weapons, not aggressive manipulation of clothing, ensuring safety and respect.

Sign of a Stimulant Overdose:

- Convulsions.
- Drowsiness.
- Calm demeanor.
- Slow breathing.

Correct Answer: Convulsions.

Explanation: Stimulant overdoses can lead to heightened bodily responses, including convulsions, due to excessive nervous system stimulation.

Not a Guideline for Conducting Patrols:

- Patrols should always follow the same method, route, and schedule.
- Vary routes and times.
- Be alert and observant.
- Engage with visitors.

Correct Answer: Patrols should always follow the same method, route, and schedule.

Explanation: Varying patrol patterns prevents predictability, enhancing effectiveness and surprise in law enforcement activities.

First Detail Given in Individual Description:

- Sex.
- Height.
- Hair color.
- Clothing.

Correct Answer: Sex.

Explanation: Providing sex first helps quickly narrow down identity in descriptions, facilitating faster recognition or search efforts.

Vehicle Search Without Warrant:

- Whenever probable cause to search exists, the search is incidental to an arrest, items are in open view through the vehicle's window.
- Only with owner's permission.
- During traffic stops.
- Randomly.

Correct Answer: Whenever probable cause to search exists, the search is incidental to an arrest, items are in open view through the vehicle's window.

Explanation: Exceptions to warrant requirements are based on immediate necessity and visible evidence, aligning with legal standards.

Least Likely Standard Item for Cycle Patrol:

- Folding shovel.
- First aid kit.
- Water bottle.
- Reflective gear.

Correct Answer: Folding shovel.

Explanation: Cycle patrols prioritize mobility and essential gear, with a folding shovel being impractical and uncommon for such patrols.

Distance for Ranger to Stay Behind Moving Vehicle:

- 50 and 75 feet.
- 10 and 20 feet.
- 100 and 150 feet.
- 25 and 35 feet.

Correct Answer: 50 and 75 feet.

Explanation: Maintaining a safe following distance ensures the ranger can react effectively while avoiding unnecessary risk during an enforcement pursuit.

Percentage of Duty Time Involving Communication:

- 75-85 percent.
- 50-60 percent.
- 20-30 percent.
- 90-100 percent.

Correct Answer: 75-85 percent.

Explanation: Communication is integral to a ranger's role, encompassing interactions with visitors, team coordination, and reporting.

Guideline for Encountering a Belligerent Offender:

- Regardless of the provocation, never exhibiting anger or impatience.
- Match their tone.
- Show impatience.
- Ignore them.

Correct Answer: Regardless of the provocation, never exhibiting anger or impatience.

Explanation: Maintaining composure de-escalates situations and ensures professional and effective handling of confrontations.

Long-Lived Evidence in Accident Scene Sketch:

- Skid marks.
- Footprints.
- Blood stains.
- Broken glass.

Correct Answer: Skid marks.

Explanation: Skid marks can persist and provide valuable insights into vehicle speed and trajectory during the accident, aiding investigations.

Best Attitude for Park Ranger:

- Service-oriented.
- Rule-focused.

- Authority-driven.
- Detached.

Correct Answer: Service-oriented.

Explanation: A service-oriented attitude prioritizes visitor experience and satisfaction, aligning with the park's mission of public enjoyment and education.

Legal Term for Surrounding Area of Visitor Abodes:

- Curtilage.
- Perimeter.
- Buffer zone.
- Exclusion zone.

Correct Answer: Curtilage.

Explanation: Curtilage refers to the area immediately surrounding a dwelling, which is afforded certain legal protections similar to the home itself.

Not a Guideline for Handling a Complaint:

- Remember that some complaints should be taken more seriously than others.
- Listen attentively.
- Address the issue promptly.
- Record details for follow-up.

Correct Answer: Remember that some complaints should be taken more seriously than others.

Explanation: All complaints should be approached with equal seriousness initially to ensure fairness and thoroughness in resolution efforts.

Guidelines for Ranger's Enforcement Actions:

- Use of physical force should be limited to the minimum necessary to implement the action, seek assistance if needed, and rule in favor of the visitor when in doubt.
- Always act alone.
- Use maximum force.
- Ignore visitor explanations.

Correct Answer: Use of physical force should be limited to the minimum necessary to implement the action, seek assistance if needed, and rule in favor of the visitor when in doubt.

Explanation: These guidelines ensure that enforcement is fair, measured, and focused on maintaining visitor trust and safety.

Primary Duty of a Park Ranger:

- Assuring each visitor a quality experience.
- Enforcing rules strictly.
- Limiting visitor access.
- Monitoring wildlife exclusively.

Correct Answer: Assuring each visitor a quality experience.

Explanation: Ensuring a positive visitor experience is key to fulfilling the park's mission of public enjoyment and appreciation of natural resources.

Not a Principle for Interpretive Services:

- The best interpretation sticks to information within the "comfort zone" of visitors.
- Engage visitors with relevant content.
- Encourage curiosity and exploration.
- Adapt to diverse visitor interests.

Correct Answer: The best interpretation sticks to information within the "comfort zone" of visitors.

Explanation: Effective interpretation challenges and expands visitor perspectives, fostering deeper understanding and appreciation.

Patrol Method with Greatest Visitor Access:

- Foot patrol.
- Vehicle patrol.
- Bicycle patrol.
- Mounted patrol.

Correct Answer: Foot patrol.

Explanation: Foot patrol allows rangers to interact directly and frequently with visitors, providing immediate assistance and information. However, it limits the ability to monitor large areas extensively.

Sign of Depressant Overdose:

- Cold, clammy skin.
- Increased heart rate.
- Hyperactivity.
- Profuse sweating.

Correct Answer: Cold, clammy skin.

Explanation: Depressants slow down the body's systems, potentially leading to symptoms like cold, clammy skin due to decreased circulation and lowered body temperature.

Common Behavior Suggesting Untruthfulness:

- Bringing the hand to the head.
- Avoiding eye contact.
- Speaking slowly.
- Smiling excessively.

Correct Answer: Bringing the hand to the head.

Explanation: This gesture can indicate stress or discomfort, often associated with deceit, as individuals unconsciously react to their own dishonesty.

Truths About Human Perception:

- People tend to overestimate the length of verticals while underestimating the width of horizontals, light-colored objects tend to be seen as heavier and nearer than dark objects of the same size and distance away, people usually recall actions and events better than objects.
- Horizontal lines are always perceived accurately.
- Dark objects are seen as closer.
- Objects and actions are recalled equally.

Correct Answer: People tend to overestimate the length of verticals while underestimating the width of horizontals, light-colored objects tend to be seen as heavier and nearer than dark objects of the same size and distance away, people usually recall actions and events better than objects.

Explanation: These perception tendencies affect how individuals report and remember events, influencing witness accounts.

Not a Criterion for DWI Refusal Consequences:

- The suspect has already completed a standard field sobriety test.
- The suspect has a history of DUI offenses.
- The suspect was driving erratically.
- The officer observed signs of intoxication.

Correct Answer: The suspect has already completed a standard field sobriety test.

Explanation: Refusal consequences hinge on refusal itself and observable intoxication signs, not prior completion of field tests.

Reading Park Map Grid Reference:

- Left to right and bottom to top.
- Top to bottom and right to left.
- Bottom to top and right to left.
- Right to left and top to bottom.

Correct Answer: Left to right and bottom to top.

Explanation: This reading order is standard for grids, ensuring consistent navigation and accurate location identification.

Defensive Opposition Level in Defense:

- Warding off blows with limbs or a baton.
- Retreating quickly.
- Shouting for help.
- Using pepper spray.

Correct Answer: Warding off blows with limbs or a baton.

Explanation: Defensive opposition involves directly countering attacks to protect oneself while minimizing aggression.

Not Part of Legal Scope of Jurisdiction:

- The park's physical boundaries.
- Federal regulations.
- State laws.
- Ranger's authority limits.

Correct Answer: The park's physical boundaries.

Explanation: Jurisdiction refers to legal authority, not physical boundaries, which are separate considerations in enforcement.

Example of "Transitional" Interpretive Experience:

- Automobile tour.

- Guided hike.

- Museum visit.

- Lecture series.

Correct Answer: Automobile tour.

Explanation: Transitional experiences facilitate movement while providing interpretive content, bridging different areas or topics.

Important Aspect for Eight-Year-Olds:

- Peer relationships are very important.

- Focus on individual tasks.

- Prefer solitary activities.

- Ignore group dynamics.

Correct Answer: Peer relationships are very important.

Explanation: At this age, children are highly influenced by peers, making group-oriented activities engaging and effective for learning.

Standard Item for Foot Patrol:

- Transceiver.

- Folding chair.

- Large backpack.

- Umbrella.

Correct Answer: Transceiver.

Explanation: A transceiver is crucial for communication, allowing foot patrol rangers to stay connected with their team and report incidents.

"Priority 3" in Enforcement Priorities:

- The protection of the park's resources from the visitor.

- Visitor safety from wildlife.

- Emergency medical response.

- Traffic management.

Correct Answer: The protection of the park's resources from the visitor.

Explanation: Ensuring that visitors do not damage or exploit park resources preserves the environment for future enjoyment and ecological balance.

Conservationist Viewpoint on Resource Management:

- Resources should be used in an essentially "as is" manner, and visitor use should blend with the resource base.

- Resources should be highly modified.

- Visitor use should be unrestricted.

- Resources should be replaced annually.

Correct Answer: Resources should be used in an essentially "as is" manner, and visitor use should blend with the resource base.

Explanation: This viewpoint emphasizes minimal alteration and sustainable interaction, aligning with ecological preservation goals.

Not a Guideline for Station Duty:

- Rangers should remain sitting or standing behind the station.
- Engage with visitors actively.
- Keep the area organized.
- Provide information proactively.

Correct Answer: Rangers should remain sitting or standing behind the station.

Explanation: Active engagement and mobility enhance visitor service and responsiveness, contrary to static positioning.

Typically False Statement About Search Warrants:

- In most situations, real estate can be seized under a search warrant.
- Warrants specify items to be seized.
- Warrants are required for private dwellings.
- Issued based on probable cause.

Correct Answer: In most situations, real estate can be seized under a search warrant.

Explanation: Search warrants focus on searching for evidence rather than seizing real estate, which involves separate legal processes.

Boundary Maintenance Responsibilities:

- Physically locating the boundary line either by previous marks or survey, identifying trespass and/or encroachment, and marking and signing the boundary.
- Patrolling the boundary daily.
- Constructing fences.
- Offering guided tours.

Correct Answer: Physically locating the boundary line either by previous marks or survey, identifying trespass and/or encroachment, and marking and signing the boundary.

Explanation: Ensuring clear and accurate boundary delineation prevents disputes and maintains park integrity.

Public Relations Program Requirements:

- Solve the problems of others while saving the problems of the park, consist of actions that are coordinated and integrated.
- Focus solely on park promotion.
- Ignore external issues.
- Operate independently.

Correct Answer: Solve the problems of others while saving the problems of the park, consist of actions that are coordinated and integrated.

Explanation: Effective public relations balance external and internal concerns, fostering positive relationships and park reputation.

Circumstances for Park Ranger Arrests:

- On an arrest warrant, on view of a felony being committed, on reasonable suspicion of a felony.

- For any minor infraction.

- Without reasonable cause.

- Only with supervisor approval.

Correct Answer: On an arrest warrant, on view of a felony being committed, on reasonable suspicion of a felony.

Explanation: Arrests require legal justification and authority, ensuring alignment with law and order principles.

Inexhaustible Natural Resource:

- Atomic energy.

- Timber.

- Freshwater.

- Soil.

Correct Answer: Atomic energy.

Explanation: Atomic energy, derived from nuclear processes, is considered inexhaustible due to its vast potential and sustainability.

Method for Maintaining Cattle Grazing Rangeland:

- Manipulating stock herds, reseeding, and firing.

- Limiting water access.

- Increasing herd size.

- Reducing grazing areas.

Correct Answer: Manipulating stock herds, reseeding, and firing.

Explanation: These practices ensure rangeland productivity and ecological balance, supporting sustainable grazing.

Advantage of Monocultural Forest Harvesting:

- Allows nurturing of shade-intolerant species.

- Promotes biodiversity.

- Reduces disease risk.

- Enhances natural regeneration.

Correct Answer: Allows nurturing of shade-intolerant species.

Explanation: Monocultural practices can optimize growth conditions for certain species, though they may reduce overall biodiversity.

Soil Type Best at Holding Water:

- Sandy clay.

- Gravel.

- Loamy sand.

- Pure sand.

Correct Answer: Sandy clay.

Explanation: Sandy clay has a balanced texture, retaining moisture effectively while allowing some drainage, ideal for plant growth.

Increase in Forest Yield Through Chipping:

- 200%.
- 50%.
- 100%.
- 150%.

Correct Answer: 200%.

Explanation: Chipping enhances resource utilization by converting waste into valuable products, significantly boosting yield.

Industry Generating Most Revenue in the U.S.:

- Cattle.
- Forestry.
- Fishing.
- Tourism.

Correct Answer: Cattle.

Explanation: The cattle industry is a major revenue generator, driven by demand for beef and dairy products, impacting agriculture significantly.

Not a Guiding Principle for Resource Conservation:

- Concentrated, singular use of particular resources.
- Sustainable management.
- Multiple-use strategies.
- Ecosystem-based planning.

Correct Answer: Concentrated, singular use of particular resources.

Explanation: Modern conservation emphasizes diverse and balanced use, avoiding over-reliance on single resources to ensure sustainability.

Soil Macronutrient:

- Calcium.
- Chlorine.
- Helium.
- Zinc.

Correct Answer: Calcium.

Explanation: Calcium is vital for plant growth, playing a crucial role in cell wall structure and nutrient uptake, classifying it as a macronutrient.

Hindrances to U.S. Food Production:

- Loss of farmland to land development, huge fossil fuel input requirement for production, transfer of water to urban populations.
- Increasing crop disease.
- Overproduction of food.
- Lack of technology.

Correct Answer: Loss of farmland to land development, huge fossil fuel input requirement for production, transfer of water to urban populations.

Explanation: These factors contribute to decreased agricultural capacity, impacting food production efficiency and sustainability.

Uses of Tree Bark:

- Medical uses, production of chemicals for tanning leather, oil-well drilling.
- Furniture construction.
- Fabric production.
- Jewelry making.

Correct Answer: Medical uses, production of chemicals for tanning leather, oil-well drilling.

Explanation: Tree bark has versatile applications, transforming a previously overlooked material into valuable resources across various industries.

Advantages of Organic Fertilizers:

- Prevention of leaching, improved soil structure, maximum aeration of root zone.
- Quick nutrient release.
- Low cost.
- Extended shelf life.

Correct Answer: Prevention of leaching, improved soil structure, maximum aeration of root zone.

Explanation: Organic fertilizers enhance soil health and sustainability by improving physical properties and nutrient retention.

Percentage of Freshwater Underground:

- 95%.
- 50%.
- 75%.
- 30%.

Correct Answer: 95%.

Explanation: A significant portion of Earth's freshwater exists underground, highlighting the importance of groundwater management and conservation.

Ocean's Contribution as a Natural Resource:

- Major source of important vitamins in the human diet.
- Unlimited energy supply.
- Endless freshwater source.
- Mineral-free water.

Correct Answer: Major source of important vitamins in the human diet.

Explanation: Oceans provide essential nutrients and vitamins through marine life, supporting global dietary needs and health.

Inexhaustible Resource with Quality Concerns:

- Solar Energy.
- Wind.

- Natural gas.
- Timber.

Correct Answer: Solar Energy.

Explanation: While solar energy is abundant, its quality can be affected by environmental pollution and inefficient technologies, impacting its utilization.

Resource Convertable to Methane Gas:

- High-Sulfur Coal.
- Timber waste.
- Agricultural residue.
- Saltwater.

Correct Answer: High-Sulfur Coal.

Explanation: High-sulfur coal can be processed to produce methane, offering an alternative energy source through chemical conversion.

Most Wasteful Use of Fossil Fuels:

- Heating.
- Transportation.
- Electricity generation.
- Industrial processes.

Correct Answer: Heating.

Explanation: Heating is often cited as wasteful due to inefficiencies and the availability of more sustainable alternatives, like geothermal and solar heating.

Best Way to Restore Soil Fertility:

- Organic fertilizers.
- Chemical pesticides.
- Frequent plowing.
- Excessive irrigation.

Correct Answer: Organic fertilizers.

Explanation: Organic fertilizers rejuvenate soil health by improving biological activity and nutrient content, promoting sustainable agriculture.

Minimum Time for Toxic Material in Groundwater:

- 200 years.
- 50 years.
- 100 years.
- 25 years.

Correct Answer: 200 years.

Explanation: Contaminants can persist in groundwater systems for extended periods, emphasizing the importance of pollution prevention and remediation.

Influential Factor in Aquatic Life Behavior:

- Temperature.
- Light availability.
- Salinity levels.
- Water depth.

Correct Answer: Temperature.

Explanation: Temperature significantly impacts metabolic rates, reproduction, and distribution of aquatic organisms, making it a crucial environmental regulator.

Consequence of Using Solar Energy:

- Decrease in photosynthetic rates of surrounding flora.
- Increased air pollution.
- Reduced energy costs.
- Noise pollution.

Correct Answer: Decrease in photosynthetic rates of surrounding flora.

Explanation: Large solar installations can alter local climates and shading, potentially affecting plant growth and ecosystems.

Coal Extraction Rate in Recent Years:

- 25 years.
- 50 years.
- 75 years.
- 10 years.

Correct Answer: 25 years.

Explanation: This rapid extraction rate underscores the intensive demand for coal and its significant role in energy production historically.

Exhaustible but Renewable Resource:

- Soil.
- Freshwater.
- Natural gas.
- Wind.

Correct Answer: Soil.

Explanation: Soil is considered renewable when managed sustainably, but it is exhaustible due to erosion and degradation from misuse.

Limiting Power of International Whaling Commission:

- Protecting certain species, deciding minimum length for permissible kill, protecting calves and nursing cows.
- Banning all whaling globally.
- Setting all catch quotas.
- Regulating fish trade.

Correct Answer: Protecting certain species, deciding minimum length for permissible kill, protecting calves and nursing cows.

Explanation: These measures aim to balance whale conservation with sustainable whaling practices, protecting vulnerable populations.

Promising Solution to Worldwide Food Shortage:

- Vigorous human population control.
- Expanding agricultural land.
- Increased use of pesticides.
- Enhanced mechanization.

Correct Answer: Vigorous human population control.

Explanation: Managing population growth addresses the root of food demand, aiming to stabilize resource consumption and improve food security.

Primary Contaminants Depleting Ozone Layer:

- Chlorinated Fluorocarbons.
- Methane emissions.
- Carbon monoxide.
- Sulfur dioxide.

Correct Answer: Chlorinated Fluorocarbons.

Explanation: Chlorinated fluorocarbons (CFCs) are synthetic compounds that break down ozone molecules, thinning the earth's protective ozone layer and increasing UV radiation exposure.

Promising Wildlife Resource Management Method:

- Habitat Development.
- Predator control.
- Species relocation.
- Hunting regulation.

Correct Answer: Habitat Development.

Explanation: Habitat development focuses on creating and restoring environments that support diverse wildlife, promoting natural population balance and ecological health.

Primary Energy Consumer in American Society:

- Industry.
- Residential homes.
- Transportation.
- Agriculture.

Correct Answer: Industry.

Explanation: Industrial processes require significant energy inputs for manufacturing, production, and operation, making it the largest energy consumer.

Percentage of Irrigation Water Absorbed by Crops:

- 25%.
- 50%.

- 75%.
- 90%.

Correct Answer: 25%.

Explanation: A substantial portion of irrigation water is lost to evaporation or runoff, with only a quarter being effectively absorbed by plant roots.

Rate of Topsoil Loss in Mississippi River:

- Fifteen tons per second.
- Ten tons per minute.
- Twenty tons per hour.
- Five tons per day.

Correct Answer: Fifteen tons per second.

Explanation: This significant soil loss highlights the challenges of soil conservation and the impact of erosion on agricultural regions.

Years Before Exhaustion of Fossil Fuels:

- 35 years.
- 50 years.
- 100 years.
- 20 years.

Correct Answer: 35 years.

Explanation: Current consumption patterns and limited reserves suggest a finite future for fossil fuels, emphasizing the need for sustainable energy solutions.

Disadvantage of Monocultural Forest Systems:

- Long harvesting rotations, runoff from intensive chemical use, creation of oversimplified ecosystems.
- Increased biodiversity.
- Enhanced natural regeneration.
- Lower disease risk.

Correct Answer: Long harvesting rotations, runoff from intensive chemical use, creation of oversimplified ecosystems.

Explanation: Monocultures can lead to ecological imbalances, dependency on chemicals, and reduced resilience against pests and diseases.

Soil Micronutrient:

- Manganese.
- Potassium.
- Nitrogen.
- Calcium.

Correct Answer: Manganese.

Explanation: Manganese is essential for plant enzyme systems and photosynthesis, though required in smaller quantities compared to macronutrients.

Increase in Per Capita Energy Consumption:

- Five times the rate of population growth.
- Equal to the population growth rate.
- Double the population growth rate.
- Half the population growth rate.

Correct Answer: Five times the rate of population growth.

Explanation: This disproportionate increase underscores the intensifying demand for energy, driven by technology and lifestyle changes.

Not a Disadvantage of Damming Rivers:

- Sedimentation of reservoirs.
- Disruption of aquatic habitats.
- Alteration of sediment flow.
- Impact on local fisheries.

Correct Answer: Sedimentation of reservoirs.

Explanation: Sedimentation is a common consequence, impacting water storage and quality, but not typically overlooked in dam assessments.

Ineffective Soil Erosion Control Method:

- Terracing.
- Contour plowing.
- Cover cropping.
- Windbreaks.

Correct Answer: Terracing.

Explanation: While terracing can be effective in certain terrains, it is not universally efficient due to varying topographies and implementation challenges.

Consumptively Used Resource with Certain Exhaustion:

- Natural Gas.
- Solar energy.
- Wind power.
- Geothermal energy.

Correct Answer: Natural Gas.

Explanation: Natural gas is finite and heavily relied upon, making its depletion inevitable without sustainable alternatives.

Sustained-Yield Harvest Program in Forestry:

- Silvicultural.
- Clear-cut.
- Shelterwood.
- Coppicing.

Correct Answer: Silvicultural.

Explanation: Silvicultural practices aim to balance forest regeneration with consistent harvests, ensuring long-term resource availability.

Annual Soil Loss in the U.S.:

- One billion tons.
- Five hundred million tons.
- Two billion tons.
- Seven hundred million tons.

Correct Answer: One billion tons.

Explanation: This staggering loss highlights the need for effective soil conservation strategies to protect agricultural productivity and ecological health.

Disadvantage of Channelization:

- Loss of hardwood timber, loss of wildlife habitat, lowering of water table.
- Improved flood control.
- Enhanced navigation.
- Increased land value.

Correct Answer: Loss of hardwood timber, loss of wildlife habitat, lowering of water table.

Explanation: Channelization can disrupt ecosystems, reduce biodiversity, and alter hydrological cycles, compromising environmental integrity.

Least Wasteful Use of Aquifer Water:

- Relieve drought.
- Support industrial processes.
- Water recreational areas.
- Maintain urban landscaping.

Correct Answer: Relieve drought.

Explanation: Using aquifer water to mitigate drought conditions prioritizes critical needs, supporting agriculture and community resilience.

Least Wasteful Use of Fossil Fuels:

- Essential liquid fuels.
- Heating.
- Electricity generation.
- Road construction.

Correct Answer: Essential liquid fuels.

Explanation: Essential liquid fuels, such as those for transportation, are critical for current infrastructure, necessitating efficient usage.

Standard Rangeland Allotment for Grazing:

- Eight acres.
- Ten acres.
- Five acres.

- Twelve acres.

Correct Answer: Eight acres.

Explanation: This measure ensures sufficient forage availability, balancing livestock needs with land sustainability.

Percentage of U.S. Forest Products for Lumber:

- 30%.
- 50%.
- 70%.
- 20%.

Correct Answer: 30%.

Explanation: A significant portion of forest products is allocated to construction and manufacturing, highlighting the importance of sustainable forestry.

Not an Influential Factor in Soil Nutrient Depletion:

- Fertilization.
- Overharvesting.
- Erosion.
- Acid rain.

Correct Answer: Fertilization.

Explanation: Fertilization replenishes nutrients, contrasting with factors that deplete soil quality, such as erosion and acid rain.

Not a Factor in Freshwater Fish Resource Decline:

- Decreasing habitat temperatures.
- Pollution.
- Overfishing.
- Habitat destruction.

Correct Answer: Decreasing habitat temperatures.

Explanation: Temperature changes can affect fish populations, but are not as direct a factor as pollution or habitat destruction in resource decline.

Effects of Oil Pollution on Marine Ecosystems:

- Introduction of carcinogens into food chain, concentration of chlorinated hydrocarbons, immediate mortality of marine animals.
- Enhanced fish breeding.
- Improved water clarity.
- Increased biodiversity.

Correct Answer: Introduction of carcinogens into food chain, concentration of chlorinated hydrocarbons, immediate mortality of marine animals.

Explanation: Oil pollution has devastating impacts on marine life, causing health issues, altering ecosystems, and reducing biodiversity.

Defensive Use of Clear-Cutting in Forestry:

- Old-growth firs of the Pacific Northwest.
- Tropical rainforests.
- Boreal forests.
- Savanna woodlands.

Correct Answer: Old-growth firs of the Pacific Northwest.

Explanation: Clear-cutting in the Pacific Northwest is sometimes used to manage old-growth forests by creating open spaces that can prevent disease spread and promote regeneration of specific tree species.

Factors Affecting Soil Erosion by Water:

- Volume of precipitation, topography of land, and type of vegetational cover.
- Soil pH, air temperature, and humidity levels.
- Soil texture, wind speed, and sunlight exposure.
- Rock type, atmospheric pressure, and root depth.

Correct Answer: Volume of precipitation, topography of land, and type of vegetational cover.

Explanation: These factors determine the speed and extent of erosion by influencing water flow, soil stability, and protective vegetation cover.

Inorganic Soil Fertilizer:

- Nitrates.
- Compost.
- Manure.
- Humus.

Correct Answer: Nitrates.

Explanation: Nitrates are synthetic compounds used to supply essential nitrogen to plants, enhancing growth and yield in agricultural systems.

Reduction of Soil Erosion on Slopes by Contour Farming:

- 30-50%.
- 10-20%.
- 60-70%.
- 80-90%.

Correct Answer: 30-50%.

Explanation: Contour farming aligns planting with land contours, reducing water runoff and soil loss by slowing erosion processes on slopes.

Vegetation Strips Surrounding Streams:

- Riparian Zones.
- Buffer Strips.
- Wetlands.
- Grasslands.

Correct Answer: Riparian Zones.

Explanation: Riparian zones are crucial for filtering runoff, stabilizing stream banks, and providing habitat for wildlife, contributing to ecosystem health.

Population with Large Reproductive Component:

- Constrictive.

- Expansive.

- Stable.

- Declining.

Correct Answer: Constrictive.

Explanation: A constrictive population has a narrower base, indicating fewer young individuals, often leading to potential future population decline.

Earliest Event in Nitrogen Cycle:

- Atmospheric nitrogen is converted by nitrogen-fixing bacteria to form usable to plants.

- Plants absorb nitrates.

- Animals consume plants.

- Decomposition of organic matter.

Correct Answer: Atmospheric nitrogen is converted by nitrogen-fixing bacteria to form usable to plants.

Explanation: Nitrogen fixation is a critical initial step, transforming inert atmospheric nitrogen into forms accessible for plant uptake and ecosystem integration.

Main Drawback of Biological Controls:

- Are slower acting and more difficult to apply.

- Are more toxic to non-target species.

- Increase resistance in pests quickly.

- Are more expensive than chemical pesticides.

Correct Answer: Are slower acting and more difficult to apply.

Explanation: Biological controls require time to establish and can be complex to implement, unlike immediate-acting chemical pesticides.

Most Important Air Pollutant for Human Health:

- Tobacco Smoke.

- Carbon monoxide.

- Ozone.

- Sulfur dioxide.

Correct Answer: Tobacco Smoke.

Explanation: Tobacco smoke is a major health risk due to its carcinogenic compounds, significantly impacting respiratory health and causing various diseases.

Compounds Contributing to Eutrophication:

- Nitrates and Phosphates.

- Chlorides and magnesium.

- Sulfates and carbonates.

- Silicates and alumina.

Correct Answer: Nitrates and Phosphates.

Explanation: These nutrients fuel excessive algae growth in water bodies, leading to oxygen depletion and ecosystem disruption, a process known as eutrophication.

Species with Broad Distribution:

- Cosmopolitan.
- Endemic.
- Indigenous.
- Invasive.

Correct Answer: Cosmopolitan.

Explanation: Cosmopolitan species thrive in diverse environments worldwide, showcasing adaptability and resilience across various ecological conditions.

Misconception about Paper Recycling:

- Creates about the same number of jobs as harvesting trees for pulp.
- Is more environmentally friendly.
- Reduces landfill waste.
- Saves energy.

Correct Answer: Creates about the same number of jobs as harvesting trees for pulp.

Explanation: Recycling paper typically requires more processing and sorting, potentially creating more jobs than traditional pulp harvesting, contrary to this statement.

Malnutrition from Weaning to Starchy Diet:

- Kwashiorkor.
- Marasmus.
- Anemia.
- Beriberi.

Correct Answer: Kwashiorkor.

Explanation: Kwashiorkor is a form of severe protein malnutrition often seen in young children who transition from breast milk to diets low in protein, leading to growth and developmental issues.

Cause of Central Europe Forest Decline:

- Acid Rain.
- Deforestation.
- Overgrazing.
- Pest infestation.

Correct Answer: Acid Rain.

Explanation: Acid rain, resulting from industrial emissions, damages foliage and soil chemistry, severely impacting tree health and vitality in sensitive forest ecosystems.

Trophic Level of Carnivores Eating Herbivores:

- Third.

- First.

- Second.

- Fourth.

Correct Answer: Third.

Explanation: In an ecosystem, primary producers form the first level, herbivores the second, and carnivores consuming herbivores occupy the third trophic level, reflecting energy transfer dynamics.

Agricultural System with High Labor Needs:

- Traditional intensive agriculture in less-developed countries.

- Industrial agriculture.

- Subsistence farming.

- Hydroponic farming.

Correct Answer: Traditional intensive agriculture in less-developed countries.

Explanation: This system relies heavily on manual labor for planting, maintenance, and harvesting, often without advanced machinery, resulting in high labor demands.

Natural Rainwater's Slight Acidity Cause:

- Carbon dioxide.

- Methane.

- Oxygen.

- Nitrogen.

Correct Answer: Carbon dioxide.

Explanation: Carbon dioxide dissolves in rainwater to form carbonic acid, giving natural rainfall a slightly acidic pH, unlike the stronger acids in acid rain.

Composition of Earth's Atmosphere:

- Free nitrogen.

- Oxygen.

- Carbon dioxide.

- Argon.

Correct Answer: Free nitrogen.

Explanation: Nitrogen makes up about 80% of Earth's atmosphere, playing a crucial role in biological processes while being largely inert in its gaseous form.

Effective Gully Reclamation Strategies:

- Building small dams, seeding with quick-growing plants, building diversion channels.

- Installing drainage pipes.

- Using chemical stabilizers.

- Applying synthetic fertilizers.

Correct Answer: Building small dams, seeding with quick-growing plants, building diversion channels.

Explanation: These strategies help stabilize soil, control water flow, and promote vegetation growth, effectively reclaiming eroded gullies.

First Nation to Adopt Population Policy:

- India.
- China.
- United States.
- Brazil.

Correct Answer: India.

Explanation: India was the first to officially implement policies aimed at controlling population growth, reflecting concerns about resource availability and economic development.

Individuals Born During Same Period:

- Cohorts.
- Generations.
- Classes.
- Groups.

Correct Answer: Cohorts.

Explanation: In demographic terms, a cohort refers to individuals born in the same time frame, used to analyze population trends and changes over time.

Full-Length Practice Test 1 (170 Q&A and Explanations)

Method to Prevent Overgrazing:

- Controlling the stocking rate.
- Rotational grazing.
- Fencing off pasture areas.
- Increasing water sources.

Correct Answer: Controlling the stocking rate.

Explanation: By managing the number of animals per unit area, the stocking rate helps maintain balance, preventing overuse of pasture resources and promoting sustainable grazing.

Non-Biological Parameters for Climax Community:

- Temperature and precipitation.
- Soil pH and altitude.
- Wind speed and solar radiation.
- Humidity and soil type.

Correct Answer: Temperature and precipitation.

Explanation: These factors critically influence the types of vegetation and animal species that can thrive, thus shaping the final stable ecosystem or climax community.

Principle of Non-Compatible Species Coexistence:

- Competitive exclusion.
- Mutualism.
- Symbiosis.
- Predation.

Correct Answer: Competitive exclusion.

Explanation: This principle posits that two species with identical needs cannot coexist indefinitely, as one will outcompete the other for limited resources, leading to exclusion.

Percentage of Medicines from Wild Plants:

- 40%.
- 20%.
- 60%.
- 10%.

Correct Answer: 40%.

Explanation: This significant percentage highlights the vital role of biodiversity in pharmaceutical development, showcasing the genetic wealth of wild plants in medicine.

Examples of Protists:

- Diatoms, slime molds, amoebas.
- Bacteria, algae, fungi.
- Yeast, molds, lichens.
- Viruses, prions, viroids.

Correct Answer: Diatoms, slime molds, amoebas.

Explanation: Protists are a diverse group of mostly unicellular organisms, including diatoms, slime molds, and amoebas, each with unique ecological roles.

Element Not in Original Environmental Impact Statement:

- Negative declaration.
- Affected environment.
- Alternatives considered.
- Environmental consequences.

Correct Answer: Negative declaration.

Explanation: The original environmental impact statement focused on assessing potential impacts and alternatives, not on issuing a negative declaration.

Energy Policy from Centralized Power Plants:

- Hard path.
- Soft path.
- Mixed approach.
- Renewable focus.

Correct Answer: Hard path.

Explanation: The hard path emphasizes large-scale, centralized energy production, often relying on non-renewable resources and extensive infrastructure.

Example of Benthic Organism:

- Sponge.
- Jellyfish.

- Tuna.
- Seagull.

Correct Answer: Sponge.

Explanation: Sponges are benthic organisms living on or near the bottom of aquatic environments, playing roles in filtering water and providing habitat.

Description of Acidic Solution:

- Any water solution that contains more hydrogen ions (H+) than hydroxide ions (OH).
- Neutral pH of 7.
- Contains more OH ions than H+ ions.
- Balanced H+ and OH ions.

Correct Answer: Any water solution that contains more hydrogen ions (H+) than hydroxide ions (OH).

Explanation: This imbalance results in an acidic pH, typical of solutions with a greater presence of H+ ions, affecting chemical reactions and biological processes.

Pioneer Community Dominant Organisms:

- Beetles.
- Mosses.
- Lichens.
- Grasses.

Correct Answer: Beetles.

Explanation: Beetles, as versatile and adaptable insects, often act as early colonizers in disturbed areas, contributing to ecosystem development and nutrient cycling.

Innermost Atmospheric Layer:

- Troposphere.
- Stratosphere.
- Mesosphere.
- Thermosphere.

Correct Answer: Troposphere.

Explanation: The troposphere is the lowest atmospheric layer, containing most of the Earth's air mass and where weather patterns occur, influencing climate and life.

Factor Not Critical for Lake Productivity:

- Proximity to marine coast.
- Nutrient levels.
- Light penetration.
- Water temperature.

Correct Answer: Proximity to marine coast.

Explanation: While coastal proximity affects salinity and ecosystems, it is not a direct determinant of freshwater lake productivity, which hinges on nutrient and light availability.

Public Opinion on Environmental Solutions:

- The development of remedial technologies.

- Government regulations.

- Community initiatives.

- Individual lifestyle changes.

Correct Answer: The development of remedial technologies.

Explanation: Many believe technological advancements are key to addressing environmental issues, offering innovative solutions for pollution control and resource management.

Forestry Term for Selective Cutting:

- Selective.

- Clear.

- Strip.

- Shelterwood.

Correct Answer: Selective.

Explanation: Selective cutting involves removing specific trees to manage forest structure, promoting ecological health and sustainable timber yield.

Pollutant Affecting Human Bones:

- Strontium 90.

- Lead.

- Mercury.

- Asbestos.

Correct Answer: Strontium 90.

Explanation: Strontium 90, a radioactive isotope, can replace calcium in bones, leading to bone cancer and other serious health issues.

Non-Obligatory Symbiotic Relationship:

- Protocooperation.

- Parasitism.

- Mutualism.

- Commensalism.

Correct Answer: Protocooperation.

Explanation: Protocooperation benefits both species involved, yet they can survive independently, unlike obligatory mutualistic interactions.

Natural Sources of Tropospheric Ozone:

- Respirating trees.

- Volcanic eruptions.

- Ocean spray.

- Soil emissions.

Correct Answer: Respirating trees.

Explanation: While trees emit volatile organic compounds contributing to ozone formation, the primary human influence is from industrial emissions.

Depletion Time for Nonrenewable Resource:

- 80%.
- 50%.
- 90%.
- 70%.

Correct Answer: 80%.

Explanation: Depletion time estimates how long a resource will last by measuring the consumption of a significant portion, indicating urgency for alternatives.

Interplanting Benefit to Farmers:

- Reduced chance of losing most or all of the year's food supply to pests or other misfortunes.
- Higher yields per acre.
- Less labor required.
- Easier pest control.

Correct Answer: Reduced chance of losing most or all of the year's food supply to pests or other misfortunes.

Explanation: Interplanting increases crop diversity, enhancing resilience against pests and environmental stresses, safeguarding food security.

Population Definition of Urban Area:

- 2500 or more.
- 5000 or more.
- 10000 or more.
- 1000 or more.

Correct Answer: 2500 or more.

Explanation: Urban areas are defined by higher population densities, impacting infrastructure, resource distribution, and environmental management.

Lake Portion with Rooted Vegetation:

- Littoral.
- Limnetic.
- Profundal.
- Benthic.

Correct Answer: Littoral.

Explanation: The littoral zone supports diverse plant life due to shallow waters and sunlight penetration, fostering rich ecosystems.

Climatic Effects of Deforestation:

- Increased temperature extremes, increased surface runoff, decreased humidity.
- Enhanced biodiversity.
- Stabilized local climate.

- Reduced soil erosion.

Correct Answer: Increased temperature extremes, increased surface runoff, decreased humidity.

Explanation: Deforestation disrupts climate regulation, leading to harsher weather conditions, altered water cycles, and diminished local humidity levels.

Unit for Radioactive Decay:

- Becquerel.
- Curie.
- Gray.
- Sievert.

Correct Answer: Becquerel.

Explanation: The Becquerel measures radioactive decay rate, indicating the activity of a radioactive source in terms of disintegrations per second.

Non-Reason for Reducing Resource Throughput:

- These methods have higher-quality energy input requirements.
- Reduced production costs.
- Improved worker safety.
- Enhanced consumer satisfaction.

Correct Answer: These methods have higher-quality energy input requirements.

Explanation: While reducing throughput improves efficiency and sustainability, requiring higher-quality energy inputs contradicts the goal of minimizing resource use and cost.

Non-Degradable Pollutant:

- Mercury.
- Organic waste.
- Paper.
- Food scraps.

Correct Answer: Mercury.

Explanation: Mercury is a heavy metal that persists in the environment, accumulating in ecosystems and posing long-term health risks due to its non-degradable nature.

Low Reproductive Rate Threatens Species:

- California Condor.
- House Sparrow.
- European Starling.
- Rock Dove.

Correct Answer: California Condor.

Explanation: The California Condor's low reproductive rate, combined with other threats, makes it vulnerable to extinction, necessitating focused conservation efforts.

Non-Difference Between Freshwater and Marine Ecosystems:

- Boundaries between freshwater ecosystems and terrestrial ecosystems are sharper.

- Salinity levels.
- Species diversity.
- Nutrient availability.

Correct Answer: Boundaries between freshwater ecosystems and terrestrial ecosystems are sharper.

Explanation: Both ecosystem types transition with varying gradients, making sharp distinctions uncommon and more context-dependent than inherent.

Region with Decreased Per Capita Grain Production:

- Sub-Saharan Africa.
- Southeast Asia.
- Latin America.
- Eastern Europe.

Correct Answer: Sub-Saharan Africa.

Explanation: Sub-Saharan Africa faces challenges such as climate change, soil degradation, and socio-economic factors impacting agricultural productivity per capita.

Different Molecular Forms in Genes:

- Alleles.
- Chromosomes.
- Nucleotides.
- Proteins.

Correct Answer: Alleles.

Explanation: Alleles are variations of a gene that arise through mutation and recombination, contributing to genetic diversity within a population.

Disadvantages of Sanitary Landfills:

- Slow breakdown of biodegradable wastes, emission of toxic gases, contamination of groundwater.
- Rapid waste decomposition.
- Low operational costs.
- Minimal land use.

Correct Answer: Slow breakdown of biodegradable wastes, emission of toxic gases, contamination of groundwater.

Explanation: These issues highlight environmental concerns associated with landfills, necessitating improved waste management and mitigation strategies.

Greatest Impact of Risk Assessment:

- Carcinogens.
- Heavy metals.
- Radioactive materials.
- Pathogens.

Correct Answer: Carcinogens.

Explanation: Risk assessment has shaped regulations around carcinogens, focusing on minimizing exposure and protecting public health from cancer risks.

Denitrification Process:

- The conversion of nitrate to molecular nitrogen.

- The fixation of atmospheric nitrogen.

- The assimilation of ammonia by plants.

- The production of nitrous oxide.

Correct Answer: The conversion of nitrate to molecular nitrogen.

Explanation: Denitrification reduces nitrate to nitrogen gas, completing the nitrogen cycle and reducing excess nutrients in ecosystems.

Current Trend for Coastal Zones:

- A single natural ecosystem requiring integration of management techniques.

- Separate management for each zone.

- Emphasis on marine life protection.

- Focus on economic development.

Correct Answer: A single natural ecosystem requiring integration of management techniques.

Explanation: Integrated management considers ecological interconnections, promoting sustainable use and conservation of coastal resources.

Efficient Method for Particulate Discharge Control:

- Electrostatic Precipitation.

- Filtration.

- Cyclonic separation.

- Incineration.

Correct Answer: Electrostatic Precipitation.

Explanation: Electrostatic precipitators efficiently capture fine particles by using electric charges, minimizing industrial air pollution.

Removal Process of Solids from Water Supply:

- Screening.

- Filtration.

- Evaporation.

- Absorption.

Correct Answer: Screening.

Explanation: Screening involves using physical barriers to remove large objects and debris from water, serving as an initial step in treatment.

Obstacles to U.S. Air Quality Control:

- High number of uncertain cause-effect relationships, resistance from industrial operations, relatively small number of particulate contaminants that have been identified.

- Strong regulatory frameworks.

- Public awareness campaigns.

- Technological advancements.

Correct Answer: High number of uncertain cause-effect relationships, resistance from industrial operations, relatively small number of particulate contaminants that have been identified.

Explanation: These challenges complicate effective air quality management, requiring ongoing research and policy adjustments to address pollutants.

Critical Step in Industrial Waste Management:

- Preliminary investigation.

- Disposal.

- Recycling.

- Treatment.

Correct Answer: Preliminary investigation.

Explanation: Understanding waste characteristics and potential impacts is crucial for developing effective management strategies that minimize environmental harm.

Non-Option for Coastal Management Control:

- Regional control based upon state collaboration.

- Federal oversight.

- Local community engagement.

- Scientific research integration.

Correct Answer: Regional control based upon state collaboration.

Explanation: While collaboration can enhance management, it is not an official option outlined by the Federal Coastal Management Program.

Process for Removing Gaseous Contaminants:

- Adsorption.

- Filtration.

- Distillation.

- Precipitation.

Correct Answer: Adsorption.

Explanation: Adsorption captures gas molecules on solid surfaces, effectively removing them from the air and improving quality.

Contaminants Catalytic Converters Address:

- Carbon monoxide, hydrocarbons, nitrogen oxides.

- Sulfur dioxide, particulate matter, lead.

- Ozone, methane, ammonia.

- Radon, asbestos, benzene.

Correct Answer: Carbon monoxide, hydrocarbons, nitrogen oxides.

Explanation: Catalytic converters reduce emissions from vehicles by converting harmful gases into less harmful substances, aiding air quality.

Chemical Wastewater Treatment Process:

- Coagulation.

- Filtration.

- Aeration.

- Sedimentation.

Correct Answer: Coagulation.

Explanation: Coagulation involves adding chemicals to clump small particles into larger ones, making them easier to remove in subsequent treatment steps.

Last Stage in Sanitary Sewage Treatment:

- Biological oxidation.

- Primary sedimentation.

- Secondary filtration.

- Sludge removal.

Correct Answer: Biological oxidation.

Explanation: Biological oxidation uses microorganisms to degrade organic matter, completing the sewage treatment process and improving effluent quality.

Unmanageable Air Quality Control Element:

- Meteorology and dispersion.

- Emission reductions.

- Pollution source identification.

- Technological innovation.

Correct Answer: Meteorology and dispersion.

Explanation: While meteorological conditions can be monitored, they cannot be controlled, influencing pollutant dispersion and air quality unpredictably.

Rationale for Water Quality Control:

- Protection of aquatic life.

- Economic development.

- Recreation enhancement.

- Industrial processes.

Correct Answer: Protection of aquatic life.

Explanation: Ensuring water quality supports healthy aquatic ecosystems, maintaining biodiversity and ecological balance crucial for environmental sustainability.

Precleaning Process in Air Quality Improvement:

- Mechanical cleaning.

- Chemical treatment.

- Electrostatic precipitation.

- Biological filtration.

Correct Answer: Mechanical cleaning.

Explanation: Mechanical cleaning involves removing large particulates from emissions, preparing the air for more precise and efficient purification methods.

Desalination Method Using Salt Filtering Membrane:

- Reverse osmosis.
- Distillation.
- Ion exchange.
- Vacuum freezing.

Correct Answer: Reverse osmosis.

Explanation: Reverse osmosis employs a semipermeable membrane to separate salt from water, providing a reliable method for desalination in water treatment.

Fundamental Criterion for Coastal Basin Management:

- Degree of water exchange or flushing rate.
- Salinity levels.
- Biodiversity index.
- Economic value.

Correct Answer: Degree of water exchange or flushing rate.

Explanation: Effective management relies on understanding and optimizing water movement, ensuring pollutant dilution and ecological health in coastal basins.

Least Desirable Heating Method for Air Release:

- Direct combustion.
- Heat exchange.
- Catalytic conversion.
- Electric heating.

Correct Answer: Direct combustion.

Explanation: Direct combustion can generate additional pollutants, making it less favorable compared to cleaner, more controlled heating methods for emissions.

First Stage of Conventional Wastewater Treatment:

- Sedimentation.
- Coagulation.
- Filtration.
- Disinfection.

Correct Answer: Sedimentation.

Explanation: Sedimentation allows solids to settle, removing large particulates early in the treatment process, setting the stage for further purification.

Air Quality Devices Removing Both Contaminants:

- Wet scrubbers.
- Electrostatic precipitators.
- Baghouse filters.
- Cyclones.

Correct Answer: Wet scrubbers.

Explanation: Wet scrubbers capture both particulate and gaseous pollutants through liquid interactions, offering versatile air cleaning capabilities.

Acceptable Restoration Process by Ecologists:

- Correct inadvertent harm or past problems.

- Achieve economic development.

- Enhance recreational areas.

- Increase agricultural output.

Correct Answer: Correct inadvertent harm or past problems.

Explanation: Restoration aims to rectify ecological damage, returning environments to functional states and promoting long-term sustainability.

Primary Removal Process for Turbidity:

- Coagulation.

- Filtration.

- Sedimentation.

- Aeration.

Correct Answer: Coagulation.

Explanation: Coagulation aggregates fine particles, facilitating their removal and reducing turbidity in water supplies, improving clarity and quality.

Objective of Chemical Removal Processes:

- Convert gases to particulate matter.

- Neutralize acidity.

- Remove toxins.

- Enhance aroma.

Correct Answer: Convert gases to particulate matter.

Explanation: This conversion allows easier capture and removal of pollutants, enhancing air purification and reducing environmental impact.

Non-Associated Practice with Silt-Polluted Basins:

- Limiting dredging to active vegetation periods.

- Planting erosion control vegetation.

- Implementing sediment traps.

- Reducing upstream silt sources.

Correct Answer: Limiting dredging to active vegetation periods.

Explanation: This approach is not typically used, as active vegetation periods need protection from disturbances to promote stability and recovery.

Standards for Municipal Water Control:

- Performance.

- Quality.

- Safety.

- Efficiency.

Correct Answer: Performance.

Explanation: Performance standards specify maximum allowable concentrations of contaminants, ensuring water safety and compliance with health regulations.

Ineffective Method for Aquifer Contamination Prevention:

- Trenching.
- Wellhead protection.
- Containment barriers.
- Monitoring wells.

Correct Answer: Trenching.

Explanation: Trenching does not effectively prevent contamination, as it may facilitate pollutant movement rather than serve as a barrier or control measure.

Non-Control Mechanism for Air Quality:

- Masking.
- Filtration.
- Adsorption.
- Catalytic conversion.

Correct Answer: Masking.

Explanation: Masking only covers odors without addressing underlying pollution, making it ineffective for genuine air quality improvement.

Process to Remove Algae or Turbidity:

- Straining.
- Filtering.
- Settling.
- Evaporation.

Correct Answer: Straining.

Explanation: Straining physically separates suspended particles from water, aiding in the removal of turbidity and improving water clarity.

Common Groundwater Treatment for Drinking Water:

- Carbon treatment.
- Chlorination.
- Distillation.
- UV irradiation.

Correct Answer: Carbon treatment.

Explanation: Carbon treatment adsorbs impurities, enhancing water quality by removing contaminants and odors commonly found in groundwater supplies.

Non-Factor in Coastal Basin Management:

- Climate.

- Water exchange rate.

- Sediment deposition.

- Biological diversity.

Correct Answer: Climate.

Explanation: While climate influences ecosystems, it is not a primary factor in coastal basin management, which focuses on water flow, sediment, and biodiversity.

Methods for Limiting Sulfur Oxide Discharge:

- Desulfurization of oil, limiting coal use to low-sulfur varieties, and removal of sulfur from coal.

- Increasing scrubber efficiency.

- Switching to natural gas.

- Implementing carbon capture.

Correct Answer: Desulfurization of oil, limiting coal use to low-sulfur varieties, and removal of sulfur from coal.

Explanation: These methods effectively reduce sulfur emissions by targeting fuel sources and chemical processes before combustion.

Non-Practice in Spoil Island Construction:

- Use of fine soil materials in construction.

- Incorporating coarse materials.

- Designing erosion-resistant surfaces.

- Creating habitat zones.

Correct Answer: Use of fine soil materials in construction.

Explanation: Fine soils are prone to erosion and instability, unsuitable for constructing durable spoil islands intended to protect marina sites.

First Step in Water Quality Control Procedure:

- Compilation of data needed to reach sound decisions about objectives.

- Implementation of treatment technologies.

- Monitoring water sources.

- Regulatory compliance review.

Correct Answer: Compilation of data needed to reach sound decisions about objectives.

Explanation: Gathering data informs objectives, enabling targeted and effective water quality management strategies.

Particulate Discharge Control Using Gravity:

- Cyclone filter.

- Electrostatic precipitator.

- Fabric filter.

- Wet scrubber.

Correct Answer: Cyclone filter.

Explanation: Cyclone filters utilize gravitational and centrifugal forces to separate particulates from air, offering a simple yet effective pollution control method.

Example of Physical Wastewater Treatment:

- Distillation.

- Biological oxidation.

- Chemical precipitation.

- Adsorption.

Correct Answer: Distillation.

Explanation: Distillation physically separates substances based on boiling points, purifying water by removing contaminants through evaporation and condensation.

Marine Environment Needing Management:

- Lagoon.

- Open ocean.

- Coral reef.

- Continental shelf.

Correct Answer: Lagoon.

Explanation: Lagoons are sensitive environments facing pressures from development and pollution, demanding focused management to preserve ecological balance.

Most Widely Used Desalinization Method:

- Distillation.

- Reverse osmosis.

- Electrodialysis.

- Freezing.

Correct Answer: Distillation.

Explanation: Distillation remains a prevalent method in the U.S., utilizing heat to separate salt from water, though newer methods are gaining popularity.

Noncrystalline Adsorbents for Air Contaminants:

- Activated carbon, silica gel, activated alumina.

- Zeolites.

- Clay minerals.

- Charcoal briquettes.

Correct Answer: Activated carbon, silica gel, activated alumina.

Explanation: These materials efficiently adsorb pollutants, offering versatile options for air purification in various industrial applications.

Guiding Practice in Shoreline Management:

- Maintaining natural drainage and stream flow.

- Constructing artificial barriers.

- Increasing recreational access.

- Expanding coastal development.

Correct Answer: Maintaining natural drainage and stream flow.

Explanation: Preserving natural hydrology supports ecological health, reducing erosion and promoting sustainable coastal zone management.

Mixing Process in Water Treatment:

- Flocculation.
- Sedimentation.
- Aeration.
- Filtration.

Correct Answer: Flocculation.

Explanation: Flocculation facilitates the clumping of particles into larger aggregates, allowing them to settle and be removed from water supplies.

Standards for Water Supply Characteristics:

- Design standards.
- Performance standards.
- Quality standards.
- Safety standards.

Correct Answer: Design standards.

Explanation: Design standards specify the physical and chemical characteristics required for municipal water supplies, ensuring consistency and safety.

Standards Defining Water Quality Approaches:

- Procedural standards.
- Operational standards.
- Technical standards.
- Regulatory standards.

Correct Answer: Procedural standards.

Explanation: Procedural standards outline methods and practices for achieving water quality, guiding consistent implementation of control measures.

Purposes of Marsh-Grass Plantings:

- Stabilizing dredge spoil, creation of marshes, and creation of alternative bulkheads.
- Enhancing aesthetic value.
- Providing recreational areas.
- Increasing commercial fishery yields.

Correct Answer: Stabilizing dredge spoil, creation of marshes, and creation of alternative bulkheads.

Explanation: These plantings support erosion control, habitat creation, and shoreline stabilization, contributing to coastal ecosystem resilience.

Non-Attempted Automotive Emissions Control:

- Modification of the conventional engine.

- Catalytic converter installation.
- Fuel composition changes.
- Exhaust gas recirculation.

Correct Answer: Modification of the conventional engine.

Explanation: While technology focuses on emission reduction systems, altering engine designs remains less commonly pursued for emissions control.

Acceptable Minimum Coastal Flow Factor:

- Dry-season low flows under natural conditions.
- Average annual rainfall.
- Peak storm surges.
- Seasonal water temperature.

Correct Answer: Dry-season low flows under natural conditions.

Explanation: Ensuring minimum flow levels prevents ecological degradation, supporting habitat stability and biodiversity in coastal ecosystems.

Primary Method for Odor Prevention in Drinking Water:

- Chlorine-ammonia treatment.
- Activated carbon filtration.
- Ozone treatment.
- UV disinfection.

Correct Answer: Chlorine-ammonia treatment.

Explanation: This method neutralizes odors by disinfecting water and controlling microbial growth, maintaining water quality and safety.

Effective Method for Containing Contaminant Leakage:

- Well pumping.
- Barrier construction.
- Chemical injection.
- Surface sealing.

Correct Answer: Well pumping.

Explanation: Pumping wells draw contaminants from groundwater, reducing plume spread and facilitating remediation of affected areas.

Ultimate Goal of 1972 Water Pollution Control Amendment:

- Total elimination of the discharge of pollutants into navigable United States water.
- Reduction of industrial discharge levels.
- Enhancement of water recreational use.
- Improvement of aquatic biodiversity.

Correct Answer: Total elimination of the discharge of pollutants into navigable United States water.

Explanation: This ambitious goal aimed to restore and maintain the integrity of the nation's waters, emphasizing pollution prevention and sustainable management.

Chemical Removal Process in Water Treatment:

- Treatment.

- Filtration.

- Sedimentation.

- Decantation.

Correct Answer: Treatment.

Explanation: Treatment involves various chemical processes to remove contaminants, enhancing water quality for safe consumption and use.

Concerns in Coastal Basin Protection:

- Changes in circulation caused by alteration of basin configuration, degradation of ecological condition of basin and its margins, loss of ecologically vital areas.

- Increasing recreational facilities.

- Expanding commercial development.

- Enhancing tourism opportunities.

Correct Answer: Changes in circulation caused by alteration of basin configuration, degradation of ecological condition of basin and its margins, loss of ecologically vital areas.

Explanation: These concerns highlight the need for careful management to preserve ecological integrity and prevent long-term damage to coastal environments.

Lime Coagulation Removes from Water Supply:

- Phosphates.

- Nitrates.

- Sulfates.

- Chlorides.

Correct Answer: Phosphates.

Explanation: Lime coagulation effectively precipitates phosphates, reducing nutrient levels and preventing eutrophication in water bodies.

Least Effective Automobile Emissions Control Method:

- Modification of liquid fuels.

- Engine tuning.

- Exhaust filtering.

- Emission monitoring.

Correct Answer: Modification of liquid fuels.

Explanation: While fuel modifications can reduce emissions, they are less effective compared to integrated technological solutions like catalytic converters.

Most Common Element in Earth's Crust by Weight:

- Oxygen.

- Silicon.

- Aluminum.

- Iron.

Correct Answer: Oxygen.

Explanation: Oxygen constitutes the largest weight percentage in Earth's crust, forming compounds like oxides and silicates essential to geological processes.

Motion of Sand Along Marine Beaches:

- Littoral drift.
- Tidal flow.
- Wave action.
- Rip currents.

Correct Answer: Littoral drift.

Explanation: Littoral drift describes the transport of sand along the coast by longshore currents, shaping beach landscapes and influencing coastal dynamics.

Consequences of Long-Term Groundwater Withdrawal:

- Lowering of water table, intrusion of saltwater into groundwater supply, compaction of porous rock by heavier upper layers.
- Increased water clarity.
- Enhanced aquifer recharge.
- Improved soil fertility.

Correct Answer: Lowering of water table, intrusion of saltwater into groundwater supply, compaction of porous rock by heavier upper layers.

Explanation: These impacts highlight the need for sustainable groundwater management to prevent resource depletion and environmental degradation.

Land Type Suffering Greatest Soil Erosion Loss:

- Cropland.
- Forest land.
- Grassland.
- Wetlands.

Correct Answer: Cropland.

Explanation: Intensive agricultural practices on cropland contribute to soil erosion, demanding conservation techniques to maintain soil health and productivity.

Fluid Material in Earth's Upper Mantle:

- Magma.
- Lava.
- Basalt.
- Granite.

Correct Answer: Magma.

Explanation: Magma is the molten rock beneath the Earth's surface, containing dissolved gases and forming the source of volcanic activity when it rises.

Porous Underground Rock for Water Source:

- Aquifer.

- Reservoir.
- Basin.
- Bedrock.

Correct Answer: Aquifer.

Explanation: Aquifers are permeable rock formations that store and transmit groundwater, supplying wells and springs with accessible water resources.

Tree Lines Reduce Soil Erosion By:

- Shielding the soil from evaporating winds.
- Increasing soil fertility.
- Enhancing water retention.
- Providing shade.

Correct Answer: Shielding the soil from evaporating winds.

Explanation: Tree lines act as windbreaks, reducing wind speed across the soil surface and minimizing erosion caused by wind-driven particle movement.

Structure to Interrupt Coastal Currents:

- Jetty.
- Breakwater.
- Sea wall.
- Groin.

Correct Answer: Jetty.

Explanation: Jetties extend into the water, trapping sand and altering currents to protect harbors and stabilize beaches against erosion.

Embankments Left by Glacial Movement:

- Moraines.
- Drumlins.
- Eskers.
- Till.

Correct Answer: Moraines.

Explanation: Moraines are accumulations of rocky debris deposited by glaciers, marking past glacial advance and retreat along their edges.

Coast Accompanying Gently Sloping Coastal Plain:

- Barrier-island coast.
- Rocky coast.
- Fjord coast.
- Cliff coast.

Correct Answer: Barrier-island coast.

Explanation: Barrier islands form parallel to flat coastal plains, providing protection against ocean waves and creating sheltered waters behind them.

Definition of Loess:

- Thick deposits of wind-transported dust.
- Volcanic ash layers.
- River sediment.
- Glacial till.

Correct Answer: Thick deposits of wind-transported dust.

Explanation: Loess is fine, silt-sized sediment deposited by wind, forming fertile soils in regions like the Midwest U.S. and parts of China.

Most Common Metallic Element in Earth's Crust:

- Aluminum.
- Iron.
- Copper.
- Zinc.

Correct Answer: Aluminum.

Explanation: Aluminum is abundant in the Earth's crust, found in minerals like bauxite, and widely used due to its lightweight and corrosion-resistant properties.

Process of One Crustal Mass Folding Under Another:

- Subduction.
- Spreading.
- Faulting.
- Folding.

Correct Answer: Subduction.

Explanation: Subduction occurs at convergent boundaries where one tectonic plate sinks beneath another, driving volcanic activity and mountain formation.

Concentration of World's Volcanic Activity:

- Islands and mountain ranges near the Pacific Rim.
- Mid-Atlantic Ridge.
- African Rift Valley.
- Himalayan Mountains.

Correct Answer: Islands and mountain ranges near the Pacific Rim.

Explanation: Known as the "Ring of Fire," this area features frequent volcanic eruptions and earthquakes due to active tectonic plate boundaries.

East-West Range of Mississippi River Drainage:

- Idaho to New York.
- California to Florida.
- Texas to Maine.
- Washington to Pennsylvania.

Correct Answer: Idaho to New York.

Explanation: The Mississippi River basin spans from the Rocky Mountains in Idaho to the Appalachian Mountains in New York, draining vast U.S. areas.

Fan-Shaped Sediment Pile at River Mouth:

- Delta.

- Alluvial fan.

- Estuary.

- Floodplain.

Correct Answer: Delta.

Explanation: Deltas form where rivers deposit sediment as they enter oceans or lakes, creating fertile land and complex ecosystems.

Area of Greatest Wave Action on Coasts:

- At the headlands.

- In the bays.

- On the beaches.

- Near the estuaries.

Correct Answer: At the headlands.

Explanation: Headlands jut into the ocean, focusing wave energy and causing erosion, while bays experience calmer water conditions.

Primary Source of Geothermal Heat:

- Gravitational compression of the earth's interior.

- Radioactive decay.

- Solar radiation.

- Ocean currents.

Correct Answer: Gravitational compression of the earth's interior.

Explanation: Earth's internal heat results from gravitational forces and radioactive decay, driving geothermal activity and plate dynamics.

Least Likely Measure to Prevent Landslides:

- Cutting a series of terraces along the slope.

- Reinforcing the slope with retaining walls.

- Improving drainage.

- Planting vegetation.

Correct Answer: Cutting a series of terraces along the slope.

Explanation: Terrace cutting may destabilize slopes, increasing landslide risk, whereas other measures enhance stability and soil retention.

Richer Low-Lying Bottom Land Made By:

- Sedimentary deposits from water runoff.

- Volcanic ash deposits.

- Glacial retreat.

- Wind deposition.

Correct Answer: Sedimentary deposits from water runoff.

Explanation: Sediments deposited by water enrich soils in lowlands, supporting agriculture and diverse ecosystems through nutrient addition.

Most Likely Cloud Form to Precipitate:

- Cumulonimbus.
- Cirrus.
- Stratus.
- Altocumulus.

Correct Answer: Cumulonimbus.

Explanation: Cumulonimbus clouds are tall, powerful formations associated with thunderstorms, heavy rain, and severe weather events.

Loss of Glacial Ice Through Melting/Evaporation:

- Ablation.
- Calving.
- Sublimation.
- Accumulation.

Correct Answer: Ablation.

Explanation: Ablation describes the reduction of glacial ice through melting and sublimation, affecting glacier mass and stability.

Definition of Igneous Rock:

- Rock that has solidified from a high-temperature molten condition.
- Rock formed by sediment compression.
- Rock altered by heat and pressure.
- Rock deposited by glacial action.

Correct Answer: Rock that has solidified from a high-temperature molten condition.

Explanation: Igneous rocks form from cooling magma or lava, comprising much of Earth's crust and varying in texture and mineral content.

Difference Between Transverse and Normal Faults:

- Plates move across each other, creating lateral friction.
- Plates collide head-on, creating vertical displacement.
- Plates slide past without vertical movement.
- Plates pull apart, causing surface tension.

Correct Answer: Plates move across each other, creating lateral friction.

Explanation: Transverse faults, or strike-slip faults, involve horizontal plate movement, leading to earthquakes without significant vertical displacement.

Precipitation From Air Mass Collision:

- Frontal.

- Orographic.
- Convectional.
- Cyclonic.

Correct Answer: Frontal.

Explanation: Frontal precipitation occurs when warm and cold air masses clash, forcing warm air to rise, cool, and condense into precipitation.

Alphabetizing Second:

- (A) flag
- (B) house
- (C) decade
- (D) emotion

Correct Answer: (D) emotion.

Explanation: When alphabetized, the order is: decade, emotion, flag, house. "Emotion" follows "decade," making it second.

Alphabetizing Fourth:

- (A) microphone
- (B) neutral
- (C) lithograph
- (D) neutron

Correct Answer: (D) neutron.

Explanation: The sequence is lithograph, microphone, neutral, neutron. "Neutron" is the fourth entry when arranged alphabetically.

Alphabetizing Third:

- (A) excitement
- (B) earnest
- (C) early
- (D) earn

Correct Answer: (B) earnest.

Explanation: The alphabetical order is: earn, early, earnest, excitement. "Earnest" comes third in this lineup.

Alphabetizing Second:

- (A) catalog
- (B) catch
- (C) carbon
- (D) curb

Correct Answer: (A) catalog.

Explanation: When ordered, it's carbon, catalog, catch, curb. "Catalog" is positioned second following "carbon."

Alphabetizing Third:

- (A) element
- (B) elephant
- (C) box
- (D) department

Correct Answer: (A) element.

Explanation: The order is: box, department, element, elephant. "Element" is third in this sequence.

Alphabetizing Third:

- (A) carton
- (B) cartographer
- (C) cart
- (D) cartoon

Correct Answer: (A) carton.

Explanation: The correct sequence is cart, carton, cartographer, cartoon. "Carton" takes the third position.

Alphabetizing Second:

- (A) polarize
- (B) omnipotent
- (C) polygraph
- (D) omniscient

Correct Answer: (D) omniscient.

Explanation: The alphabetical order is: omnipotent, omniscient, polarize, polygraph. "Omniscient" is second.

Alphabetizing Fourth:

- (A) Walsh, Carol C.
- (B) Walter, Henry Delano
- (C) Walsh, Joseph C.
- (D) Walsheim, Joe

Correct Answer: (B) Walter, Henry Delano.

Explanation: The order is: Walsh, Carol C.; Walsheim, Joe; Walsh, Joseph C.; Walter, Henry Delano. "Walter, Henry Delano" is fourth.

Alphabetizing Third:

- (A) McDonough, Kevin
- (B) McDonohugh, K.
- (C) Da Costa, Hector
- (D) Costa, Hector David

Correct Answer: (B) McDonohugh, K.

Explanation: In order: Costa, Hector David; Da Costa, Hector; McDonohugh, K.; McDonough, Kevin. "McDonohugh, K." is third.

Alphabetizing Fourth:

- (A) Albers, J. A.
- (B) Albers, John Anthony
- (C) Sorensen, Edward J.
- (D) Sorensen, Ed Joseph

Correct Answer: (C) Sorensen, Edward J.

Explanation: The alphabetical sequence is: Albers, J. A.; Albers, John Anthony; Sorensen, Ed Joseph; Sorensen, Edward J. "Sorensen, Edward J." is fourth.

Alphabetizing Second:

- (A) Smith, Joan
- (B) Smith, Joan J.
- (C) Smith, J.
- (D) Smithers, J.

Correct Answer: (A) Smith, Joan.

Explanation: The order is: Smith, J.; Smith, Joan; Smith, Joan J.; Smithers, J. "Smith, Joan" is second.

Alphabetizing Third:

- (A) Read-i-mart
- (B) Ready Steady Office Supplies
- (C) Read for Life Program
- (D) Red Robin Trucking

Correct Answer: (B) Ready Steady Office Supplies.

Explanation: The sequence is: Read for Life Program, Read-i-mart, Ready Steady Office Supplies, Red Robin Trucking. "Ready Steady Office Supplies" is third.

Alphabetizing Fourth:

- (A) Henry Miller and Sons
- (B) Millerton Quarry
- (C) The Mill on the Hill
- (D) Haven Salon

Correct Answer: (B) Millerton Quarry.

Explanation: In order: Haven Salon, Henry Miller and Sons, The Mill on the Hill, Millerton Quarry. "Millerton Quarry" is fourth.

Alphabetizing Second:

- (A) 11th Street Gym
- (B) Rayson Railroad Company
- (C) Ray's Diner
- (D) Evanston Auto Parts

Correct Answer: (D) Evanston Auto Parts.

Explanation: The order is: 11th Street Gym, Evanston Auto Parts, Ray's Diner, Rayson Railroad Company. "Evanston Auto Parts" is second.

Alphabetizing Fourth:

- (A) East Bay Records
- (B) Garrett Van Buren, Ltd
- (C) Eastern Construction
- (D) Van-B-Mine Auto Rentals

Correct Answer: (B) Garrett Van Buren, Ltd.

Explanation: The sequence is: East Bay Records, Eastern Construction, Van-B-Mine Auto Rentals, Garrett Van Buren, Ltd. "Garrett Van Buren, Ltd." is fourth.

Letter As Far After E as Q After H:

- (A) M
- (B) N
- (C) O
- (D) D

Correct Answer: (B) N.

Explanation: Q is 9 letters after H, and similarly, N is 9 letters after E in the alphabet.

Letter as Far After C as T is After A:

- (A) R
- (B) U
- (C) V
- (D) X

Correct Answer: (C) V.

Explanation: T is 19 letters from A, and similarly, V is 19 letters from C in the alphabet.

Letter as Far Before L as O is Before Z:

- (A) A
- (B) B
- (C) W
- (D) X

Correct Answer: (A) A.

Explanation: O is 12 letters before Z, and A is 12 letters before L in the alphabet.

Letter as Far Before V as X After P:

- (A) L
- (B) M
- (C) N
- (D) O

Correct Answer: (C) N.

Explanation: X is 8 letters after P, and N is 8 letters before V in the alphabet.

Letter as Far After I as R is After G:

- (A) T
- (B) U
- (C) V
- (D) X

Correct Answer: (A) T.

Explanation: R is 11 letters after G, and T is 11 letters after I in the alphabet.

Letter as Far Before J as K is After B:

- (A) C
- (B) B
- (C) A
- (D) U

Correct Answer: (C) A.

Explanation: K is 9 letters after B, and A is 9 letters before J in the alphabet.

Letter as Far Before U as T is After J:

- (A) J
- (B) K
- (C) L
- (D) M

Correct Answer: (B) K.

Explanation: T is 10 letters after J, and K is 10 letters before U in the alphabet.

Letter as Far After Q as J is After E:

- (A) V
- (B) W
- (C) X
- (D) Y

Correct Answer: (A) V.

Explanation: J is 5 letters after E, and V is 5 letters after Q in the alphabet.

Letter as Far Before N as X is After S:

- (A) R
- (B) S
- (C) I
- (D) J

Correct Answer: (C) I.

Explanation: X is 5 letters after S, and I is 5 letters before N in the alphabet.

Letter as Far After E as K is Before R:

- (A) H

- (B) I
- (C) J
- (D) L

Correct Answer: (D) L.

Explanation: K is 7 letters before R, and L is 7 letters after E in the alphabet.

Address Check - Correct Error Type:

- (A) No Errors
- (B) Address Only
- (C) ZIP Code Only
- (D) Both

Correct Answer: (C) ZIP Code Only.

Explanation: The ZIP code error is evident as 62571 is correct, but 65271 is listed erroneously.

Address Check - Correct Error Type:

- (A) No Errors
- (B) Address Only
- (C) ZIP Code Only
- (D) Both

Correct Answer: (B) Address Only.

Explanation: The address is incorrect with "Conners" instead of "Conyers," while the ZIP code remains accurate.

Address Check - Correct Error Type:

- (A) No Errors
- (B) Address Only
- (C) ZIP Code Only
- (D) Both

Correct Answer: (C) ZIP Code Only.

Explanation: The ZIP code should be 30707, not 30307, indicating a typographical error in the postal code.

Address Check - Correct Error Type:

- (A) No Errors
- (B) Address Only
- (C) ZIP Code Only
- (D) Both

Correct Answer: (D) Both.

Explanation: Both the address ("Champaine" vs. "Champlaine") and the ZIP code (24101 vs. 42101) contain discrepancies.

Address Check - Correct Error Type:

- (A) No Errors
- (B) Address Only

- (C) ZIP Code Only
- (D) Both

Correct Answer: (A) No Errors.

Explanation: The address and ZIP code match perfectly, indicating no mistakes in the listed information.

Identical Letter Pairs:

- HIFGDA HIFGDA
- PEWHEI PEWHEI
- UENGSO UEGNSO
- MBDHEK MBDHEK
- PQNGGD PQNGGD
- OIEMGH OIEMGH

Correct Answer: (C) 5.

Explanation: The pairs HIFGDA, PEWHEI, MBDHEK, PQNGGD, and OIEMGH are identical, making five pairs exactly alike.

Identical Letter Pairs:

- ehgsoe ehgsoe
- ththet ththet
- lmqbts lmbqts
- kehgng kehgng
- lmqyeo lmqyeo
- jqzdue jqdzue

Correct Answer: (B) 4.

Explanation: The pairs ehgsoe, ththet, kehgng, and lmqyeo are identical, resulting in four pairs that are exactly alike.

Identical Number Pairs:

- 836459 834659
- 916533 916353
- 264821 268421
- 163943 169343
- 012039 021039
- 936129 936129

Correct Answer: (B) 1.

Explanation: Only the pair 936129 is exactly alike, resulting in one identical pair.

Identical Letter Pairs:

- JHEISH JHEISH
- KEIWNE KEIWNE
- OENMZN OEMNZN

- MKENSH MKENSH
- BEVWE BEWVE
- JIHNEM JIHNEM

Correct Answer: (C) 4.

Explanation: The pairs JHEISH, KEIWNE, MKENSH, and JIHNEM are identical, totaling four pairs that match exactly.

Identical Number Pairs:

- 821421 821241
- 726191 726191
- 827015 820715
- 287651 287651
- 009824 008924
- 721182 721182

Correct Answer: (C) 3.

Explanation: The pairs 726191, 287651, and 721182 are identical, making three pairs exactly alike.

Identical Letter Pairs:

- aebjhg aebjhg
- amanej amanej
- kejqez keqjez
- ikeplo ikpelo
- nmesda mnesda
- wierew wierew

Correct Answer: (D) 3.

Explanation: The pairs aebjhg, amanej, and wierew are identical, resulting in three pairs that match exactly.

Identical Number Pairs:

- 902711 902711
- 764201 764201
- 434309 434309
- 189361 189361
- 547789 547789
- 882718 882718

Correct Answer: (D) 6.

Explanation: All pairs are identical, resulting in six pairs that are exactly alike.

Identical Letter Pairs:

- GIHEKE GIHEKE
- KIWNEB KWINEB
- PQMZJI PQMZIJ

- MENTWN METNWN

- OPZIBS OPZIBS

- PONEHE POENHE

Correct Answer: (C) 2.

Explanation: The pairs GIHEKE and OPZIBS are identical, resulting in two identical pairs.

Identical Letter Pairs:

- jehowe jehowe

- nwkebt nwekbt

- ojejerj okejii

- nleotn nelotn

- lnwezb lnewzb

- nqwerj nwqeri

Correct Answer: (B) 1.

Explanation: Only the pair jehowe is identical, resulting in one identical pair.

Identical Number Pairs:

- 278126 278126

- 901272 902172

- 826482 824682

- 004657 004657

- 128532 125832

- 278917 278971

Correct Answer: (C) 2.

Explanation: The pairs 278126 and 004657 are identical, making two pairs exactly alike.

Repeated Letters in INVOLUNTARILY:

- (A) 0

- (B) 1

- (C) 2

- (D) 3

Correct Answer: (D) 3.

Explanation: The letters 'I', 'N', and 'L' appear more than once in the word INVOLUNTARILY.

Words Without Repeated Letters:

- (A) 11

- (B) 12

- (C) 13

- (D) 14

Correct Answer: (C) 13.

Explanation: In the sentence, 13 words contain letters that do not repeat within the word itself, such as "It," "was," and "me."

Numbers Used More Than Twice:

- 1875327862190162846214123
- (A) 3
- (B) 4
- (C) 5
- (D) 6

Correct Answer: (B) 4.

Explanation: In the sequence, the numbers '1', '2', '6', and '8' each appear more than twice, totaling four such numbers.

Letters Used More Than Once:

- IMMEASURABLE
- (A) 1
- (B) 2
- (C) 3
- (D) 4

Correct Answer: (C) 3.

Explanation: The letters 'M', 'E', and 'A' appear more than once in the word IMMEASURABLE, totaling three repeated letters.

Words with Repeated Letters:

- "It is strongly recommended that you made a reservation prior to arriving at the restaurant."
- (A) 4
- (B) 5
- (C) 6
- (D) 7

Correct Answer: (C) 6.

Explanation: The words "strongly," "recommended," "reservation," "arriving," "restaurant," and "made" contain letters that repeat within them, totaling six.

Times 2 Comes After 3 and After an Even Number:

- 1326832160518932316453210423218 7
- (A) 0
- (B) 1
- (C) 2
- (D) 3

Correct Answer: (B) 1.

Explanation: In the sequence, '2' follows '3' and '3' follows an even number only once.

Letters Used More Than Once:

- LUMBERING
- (A) 0
- (B) 1
- (C) 2
- (D) 3

Correct Answer: (A) 0.

Explanation: In the word LUMBERING, no letter appears more than once.

Times 6 Comes Before 5 and 5 Before an Odd Number:

- 21365657065265 8965326932165976
- (A) 0
- (B) 1
- (C) 2
- (D) 3

Correct Answer: (D) 3.

Explanation: The sequence '6' followed by '5' and '5' followed by an odd number occurs three times in the string.

Numbers Used More Than Three Times:

- 01278216743218649 1237289167298
- (A) 0
- (B) 2
- (C) 4
- (D) 6

Correct Answer: (C) 4.

Explanation: The numbers '1', '2', '8', and '7' appear more than three times in the sequence, totaling four such numbers.

Words with Repeated Letters:

- "Attempting to renovate a historical building can be challenging both physically and financially."
- (A) 4
- (B) 5
- (C) 6
- (D) 7

Correct Answer: (D) 7.

Explanation: The words "attempting," "renovate," "historical," "challenging," "physically," "financially," and "building" contain letters that repeat, totaling seven.

Purpose of Civil Service:

- (A) Create a merit-based system

- (B) Establish uniform methods of practice and procedure
- (C) Ensure fair employment practices
- (D) Provide public services efficiently

Correct Answer: (B) Establish uniform methods of practice and procedure.

Explanation: The civil service aims to create standardized procedures to ensure consistency and efficiency in government operations.

Timing and Location of Civil Service Meetings:

- (A) 10:00 every 1st Monday of the month at City Hall
- (B) 9:30 every 3rd Tuesday of the month at City Council Chambers
- (C) 2:00 every 2nd Wednesday of the month at Municipal Building
- (D) 11:00 every 4th Thursday of the month at Civic Center

Correct Answer: (B) 9:30 every 3rd Tuesday of the month at City Council Chambers.

Explanation: Meetings are held at this specific time and location to facilitate regular scheduling and attendance.

Guide for the Commission:

- (A) State Government Guidelines
- (B) Internal Policies and Procedures
- (C) Robert's "Rules of Order"
- (D) Federal Regulations

Correct Answer: (C) Robert's "Rules of Order".

Explanation: These rules provide a structured framework for conducting meetings and making decisions, ensuring orderly and fair proceedings.

Composition of Commission Staff:

- (A) Only the Chief Examiner
- (B) Chief Examiner and Board Members
- (C) Chief Examiner and such assistants and employees as may be required
- (D) Only elected officials

Correct Answer: (C) Chief Examiner and such assistants and employees as may be required.

Explanation: This composition ensures that the commission has the necessary personnel for efficient operation.

Filing of Additions and Amendments:

- (A) Must be verbally communicated to the Chairperson
- (B) Must be in writing and submitted electronically
- (C) Must be in writing and filed with the Secretary of the Commission
- (D) Can be filed informally at meetings

Correct Answer: (C) Must be in writing and filed with the Secretary of the Commission.

Explanation: This ensures that changes are formally documented and accessible for record-keeping and reference.

Timeline for Amendments or Additions:

- (A) 5 days prior to the action
- (B) 7 days prior to the action
- (C) 10 days prior to the action
- (D) 14 days prior to the action

Correct Answer: (C) 10 days prior to the action.

Explanation: This timeframe allows for adequate review and preparation before implementing any changes.

Frequency of Classification Review:

- (A) Annually
- (B) Every 2 years
- (C) Every 3 years
- (D) Every 5 years

Correct Answer: (B) Every 2 years.

Explanation: Regular reviews ensure that classifications remain relevant and accurate, adapting to any changes in roles or responsibilities.

Responsible for Classification Review:

- (A) Human Resources Department
- (B) Labor and Management
- (C) External Consultants
- (D) Board of Directors

Correct Answer: (B) Labor and Management.

Explanation: These parties collaborate to ensure that classification systems are fair and reflective of the workforce's needs and dynamics.

Purpose of the Regulation (Sec 143.001):

- (A) To ensure efficient public services with temporary employment
- (B) To maintain effective fire and police departments with qualified personnel, free from political interference, with stable employment
- (C) To secure efficient fire and police departments with temporary staff
- (D) To develop political influence in fire and police departments

Correct Answer: (B) To maintain effective fire and police departments with qualified personnel, free from political interference, with stable employment.

Explanation: The regulation aims to establish well-functioning fire and police departments by employing competent staff who are protected from political pressures and have job security.

Coverage of the Regulation (Sec 143.002):

- (A) Cities with a population of 5,000 or more
- (B) Municipalities with a population of 10,000 or more, having a paid fire/police department, and having voted to adopt this chapter
- (C) All municipalities regardless of population
- (D) Only cities with volunteer fire/police departments

Correct Answer: (B) Municipalities with a population of 10,000 or more, having a paid fire/police department, and having voted to adopt this chapter.

Explanation: The chapter applies to municipalities meeting the specified population and departmental criteria, ensuring appropriate governance.

Population Determination:

- (A) State census only
- (B) Federal decennial census and annual population estimates by the state demographer if more recent
- (C) Local surveys
- (D) None of these

Correct Answer: (B) Federal decennial census and annual population estimates by the state demographer if more recent.

Explanation: Population figures are determined by the most current federal or state data, ensuring up-to-date applicability of the chapter.

Definitions (Sec 143.003):

- (A) Commission refers to the police department
- (B) Department head means chief or head of the police/fire department
- (C) Director refers to city mayor
- (D) Firefighter applies to all city employees

Correct Answer: (B) Department head means chief or head of the police/fire department.

Explanation: Definitions clarify roles and responsibilities within the civil service framework, such as the department head being the chief of the respective department.

Election to Adopt/Repeal (Sec 143.004):

- (A) Election held every six months
- (B) Election held on the first authorized date post-petition with 10% voter signatures
- (C) Petition requires 50% voter signatures
- (D) No election needed for adoption or repeal

Correct Answer: (B) Election held on the first authorized date post-petition with 10% voter signatures.

Explanation: The process for adopting or repealing the chapter is initiated by a voter petition, ensuring democratic involvement.

CHAPTER 8
MASTERING THE ORAL INTERVIEW

Preparing for the Interview Process

The oral interview is a crucial component of the civil service exam, designed to assess not only your knowledge and expertise but also your communication skills, demeanor, and suitability for the role. Preparing for this stage requires a strategic approach that combines thorough research, self-awareness, and practice. Mastering the interview process can significantly enhance your chances of success and pave the way for a rewarding career in public service.

Begin by understanding the specific requirements and expectations of the role for which you are applying. Each civil service position has unique competencies and criteria that the interview panel will be evaluating. Familiarize yourself with the job description, focusing on key responsibilities and the skills necessary to perform them effectively. This knowledge will allow you to tailor your responses to align with what the interviewers are seeking.

Research the organization or department you hope to join. Understanding its mission, values, and current initiatives provides context and demonstrates your genuine interest in becoming a part of the team. Being informed about recent developments or challenges faced by the department can also help you craft insightful questions and responses that reflect your engagement with the broader goals of the organization.

Self-assessment is a critical step in preparing for the oral interview. Reflect on your personal strengths and weaknesses, and consider how they relate to the position. Identify specific experiences or achievements that highlight your abilities and demonstrate your potential as a candidate. Prepare to discuss these examples in detail, using the STAR method (Situation, Task, Action, Result) to structure your responses. This framework helps convey your thought process and the impact of your actions clearly and concisely.

Practice is essential for building confidence and refining your communication skills. Conduct mock interviews with friends, family, or mentors, simulating the interview environment as closely as possible. Use feedback from these sessions to improve your delivery, ensuring that you articulate your thoughts clearly and present yourself professionally. Pay attention to non-verbal communication, such as eye contact, posture, and gestures, as these cues play a significant role in conveying confidence and engagement.

Anticipate potential questions that may arise during the interview. These could range from inquiries about your qualifications and work experience to situational questions designed to assess your problem-solving abilities and decision-making skills. Prepare thoughtful and relevant responses, but be careful to avoid memorization. The goal is to speak naturally and authentically, demonstrating your ability to think on your feet.

Developing effective listening skills is another crucial aspect of interview preparation. An interview is a two-way conversation, and active listening shows respect and attentiveness to the interviewers. Practice paraphrasing or summarizing questions to ensure understanding before responding. This technique not only confirms that you have grasped the question but also gives you a moment to organize your thoughts.

Prepare insightful questions to ask the interview panel. Thoughtful questions demonstrate your interest in the role and your proactive approach to understanding the department's needs and challenges. Consider asking about team dynamics, opportunities for professional development, or specific projects you might be involved in. These inquiries can provide valuable insights into the position and help you assess whether it aligns with your career goals.

Managing interview anxiety is crucial for maintaining composure and delivering your best performance. Techniques such as deep breathing, visualization, or positive self-talk can help calm nerves and boost confidence. It is also helpful to envision the interview as a conversation rather than an interrogation, focusing on the opportunity to share your experiences and learn about the organization.

Attention to detail in logistics is essential to ensure a smooth interview experience. Confirm the interview time and location well in advance, and plan your route to avoid any last-minute stress. Dress appropriately for the role, adhering to professional standards that reflect the department's culture. Arriving early demonstrates punctuality and gives you time to settle and collect your thoughts before the interview begins.

Effective Body Language

Effective body language during the oral interview of the civil service exam plays a pivotal role in creating a strong impression. This non-verbal communication can convey confidence, professionalism, and engagement, often speaking louder than words. Mastering the subtleties of body language enhances your ability to connect with the interview panel and reinforces the verbal content of your responses.

Understanding the significance of eye contact is fundamental. Maintaining appropriate eye contact conveys confidence and attentiveness. It signals to the interviewers that you are engaged and interested in the conversation. However, it is important to strike a balance; too much eye contact can feel intense, while too little may come off as disinterest. Aim to make consistent eye contact with each panel member, shifting naturally as you respond to questions.

Your posture speaks volumes about your confidence and readiness. Sitting up straight with shoulders back exudes professionalism and self-assuredness. It demonstrates that you take the interview seriously and are prepared to engage fully. Avoid slouching or leaning back excessively, as these positions can convey a lack of interest or energy. A strong posture sets the tone for the interaction and aligns with the image of competence you wish to project.

Gestures are another key component of effective body language. When used appropriately, gestures can reinforce your verbal messages and add emphasis to key points. They should be natural and purposeful, complementing rather than distracting from your words. Avoid excessive or erratic movements, as they can detract from your message. Instead, use gestures sparingly to highlight important ideas and convey enthusiasm.

Facial expressions are powerful conveyors of emotion and intent. A genuine smile can create a welcoming atmosphere and help build rapport with the interviewers. It conveys positivity and openness, making you appear approachable and personable. However, be mindful of your expressions throughout the interview; ensure they align with the tone of your responses and the topic being discussed. Consistent, appropriate facial expressions demonstrate emotional intelligence and the ability to connect with others.

The use of nodding can signal agreement and understanding. It shows that you are actively listening and processing the information being shared. A slight nod when an interviewer is speaking can encourage open dialogue and show that you value their input. However, be cautious not to overuse this gesture, as excessive nodding can seem insincere or overly eager.

Hand placement is a subtle but significant aspect of body language. Keeping your hands visible and resting them gently on the table or in your lap can convey openness and honesty. Avoid crossing your arms, as this can create a barrier and suggest defensiveness. Similarly, placing hands in pockets or fidgeting can indicate nervousness. Maintaining calm and controlled hand placement supports the image of composure and professionalism.

Mirroring the body language of the interviewers, when done subtly, can foster a sense of connection and rapport. This technique involves reflecting the posture, tone, or gestures of the panel in a natural manner. It creates a sense of harmony and can make the interaction feel more collaborative. Be mindful, however, to avoid mimicry, as it should come across as genuine and not forced.

Awareness of personal space is crucial in maintaining comfort and respect in the interview setting. Respecting the physical boundaries of the interview space is important, as invading personal space can lead to discomfort. Position yourself at an appropriate distance, allowing room for natural interaction without encroaching on the interviewers' space. This respect for boundaries demonstrates professionalism and awareness of social cues.

Pausing strategically in your verbal responses can be enhanced with supportive body language, such as a thoughtful gaze or slight hand gesture. These pauses allow you to gather your thoughts and convey confidence in your ability to articulate well-considered responses. They also provide the interviewers with a moment to digest your words, creating a balanced rhythm in the conversation.

Answering Behavioral Questions

Navigating the landscape of behavioral questions during the civil service oral interview demands a blend of introspection, articulation, and strategy. These questions are designed to delve into your past experiences to predict future behavior, assessing competencies such as problem-solving, teamwork, adaptability, and leadership. Mastering the art of responding to behavioral inquiries not only enhances your candidacy but also highlights your potential as a valuable asset in public service.

Behavioral questions often start with prompts like "Tell me about a time when..." or "Give an example of how you...," inviting you to share specific instances from your professional or personal life. The STAR method—Situation, Task, Action, Result—serves as an effective framework for structuring your responses. This method ensures your answers are clear, concise, and demonstrate a logical progression of thought.

Begin by setting the stage with the Situation. Provide context by describing the scenario or challenge you faced. This introduction should be succinct yet detailed enough to give the interviewers a clear understanding of the circumstances. Avoid unnecessary background information that detracts from the core of your story. Instead, focus on the relevant aspects that set the scene for your actions.

Next, define the Task, clarifying your role and responsibilities within the situation. This step highlights your involvement and sets the stage for the actions you took. Clearly articulating your role is crucial, as it distinguishes your contributions from those of others involved in the scenario. Ensure that the task relates directly to the competencies the interviewers are assessing.

The Action component is the heart of your response, detailing the steps you took to address the challenge or achieve the objective. Describe your actions in a logical sequence, emphasizing the decision-making process, the skills you employed, and any obstacles you overcame. This part of your answer should showcase your initiative, creativity, and problem-solving abilities. Be specific about your contributions, as vague descriptions can weaken the impact of your response.

Conclude with the Result, illustrating the outcome of your actions. Highlight the positive impact of your efforts, using quantifiable data or specific achievements whenever possible. This demonstrates the value of your contributions and provides concrete evidence of your effectiveness. If the outcome was not entirely successful, be honest and reflect on what you learned from the experience, emphasizing your capacity for growth and improvement.

Preparation is key to answering behavioral questions confidently. Begin by reflecting on your past experiences, identifying examples that align with the competencies required for the role. Consider diverse scenarios from different aspects of your life, including work, volunteer activities, or academic projects. This variety ensures you have a rich pool of experiences to draw from during the interview.

Practice articulating your responses using the STAR method, either through mock interviews or self-reflection. Rehearsing aloud can help refine your delivery, ensuring that your answers are coherent and impactful. Recording your practice sessions provides an opportunity to review and adjust your responses, focusing on clarity and conciseness.

While preparation is essential, avoid memorizing responses verbatim. The goal is to speak naturally and authentically, adapting your examples to fit the specific question posed by the interviewers. Flexibility in your responses demonstrates your ability to think critically and communicate effectively under pressure.

Active listening is crucial in understanding the nuances of each behavioral question. Pay close attention to the wording, ensuring you grasp the specific competency being assessed. This awareness allows you to tailor your response to directly address the question, providing relevant examples that highlight your strengths.

If a question catches you off guard, take a moment to gather your thoughts before responding. It is acceptable to pause briefly to organize your ideas, demonstrating your composure and ability to think on your feet. If necessary, ask for clarification to ensure you fully understand the question, showing your commitment to providing a thoughtful and accurate response.

Throughout the interview, maintain a positive and professional demeanor. Even when discussing challenging situations or setbacks, focus on the constructive aspects of your experience. Highlight the skills and qualities you demonstrated, emphasizing resilience, adaptability, and a proactive approach to problem-solving.

The STAR Technique

Harnessing the STAR technique for the civil service oral interview is a powerful strategy for delivering structured and impactful responses. This technique—encompassing Situation, Task, Action, and Result—enables candidates to articulate their experiences clearly and effectively, showcasing their competencies and potential to thrive in a public service role. Understanding and mastering this approach can significantly enhance your performance during the interview process.

The "Situation" component serves as the foundation for your response. Begin by describing the context or challenge you encountered, setting the stage for the actions you took. This part of your answer should be concise yet informative, providing just enough detail to engage the interviewers without overwhelming them with extraneous information. The goal is to paint a clear picture of the scenario, allowing the panel to understand the backdrop against which you acted.

Following the situation, delineate the "Task." Clearly outline your specific role or responsibility within this context. This step is crucial for establishing your involvement and the expectations placed upon you. It distinguishes your contributions from those of others, framing the narrative around your actions and decisions. By clearly defining the task, you provide a focal point for the interviewers, guiding them through your thought process and approach to the challenge.

Transition smoothly into the "Action" phase, where you detail the steps you took to address the situation or fulfill the task. This section should be the most detailed part of your response, as it highlights your problem-solving abilities, initiative, and critical thinking skills. Discuss the strategies you employed, the decisions you made, and the obstacles you overcame. Be specific and articulate, using vivid language to convey the impact of your actions. This is your opportunity to demonstrate your capabilities and the value you bring to the table.

Conclude with the "Result," showcasing the outcome of your efforts. Wherever possible, quantify your achievements or provide specific examples that illustrate the success of your actions. Highlight the positive impact on your team, organization, or personal growth, offering tangible evidence of your effectiveness. When outcomes were not as expected, reflect on the lessons learned and how you applied these insights to future situations. This demonstrates growth and adaptability, reinforcing your readiness for a civil service role.

Preparation is key to effectively utilizing the STAR technique. Begin by reflecting on your past experiences, identifying examples that align with the competencies required for the position. Choose scenarios that demonstrate a range of skills and qualities, such as leadership, teamwork, adaptability, and communication. This diversity ensures you have a rich pool of experiences to draw from during the interview.

Practicing your responses is essential for refining your delivery. Engage in mock interviews with peers or mentors, focusing on structuring your answers using the STAR method. Record these sessions if possible, reviewing them to assess clarity, conciseness, and impact. Feedback from others can provide valuable insights into areas for improvement, helping you hone your skills and build confidence.

While preparation is crucial, avoid memorizing responses. The aim is to speak naturally and authentically, adapting your examples to fit the specific questions posed by the interviewers. This flexibility demonstrates your ability to think critically and communicate effectively under pressure, qualities highly valued in public service roles.

Active listening is vital for understanding the nuances of each interview question. Pay close attention to the wording, ensuring you grasp the specific competency being assessed. This awareness allows you to tailor your response to directly address the question, providing relevant examples that highlight your strengths and achievements.

If you encounter a question that challenges you, take a moment to gather your thoughts before responding. It is acceptable to pause briefly to organize your ideas, demonstrating composure and the ability to think on your feet. If necessary, ask for clarification to ensure you fully understand the question, showing your commitment to providing a thoughtful and accurate response.

Throughout the interview, maintain a positive and professional demeanor. Even when discussing challenging situations or setbacks, focus on the constructive aspects of your experience. Highlight the skills and qualities you demonstrated, emphasizing resilience, adaptability, and a proactive approach to problem-solving.

Remember, the STAR technique is not just a tool for structuring responses; it is a method for showcasing your unique qualities and experiences. It allows you to differentiate yourself from other candidates by illustrating your personal contributions and the impact you have made in various contexts. By preparing thoroughly and responding strategically, you can effectively convey your potential to excel in a civil service role.

Mock Interview Scenarios

Preparing for the civil service oral interview can be greatly enhanced by engaging in mock interview scenarios. This practice allows candidates to simulate the interview environment, refine their responses, and build confidence. By immersing themselves in realistic situations, individuals can identify areas for improvement and hone the skills necessary to succeed in the actual interview. The following exploration of mock interview scenarios provides a roadmap for effective preparation.

Crafting a range of scenarios is essential to cover the diverse questions that might arise during the interview. Begin by considering the competencies required for the position, such as leadership, problem-solving, communication, and adaptability. Develop hypothetical situations that reflect these competencies, ensuring that each scenario is challenging yet relevant. This breadth of scenarios ensures that candidates are well-prepared to address various aspects of the role.

In one scenario, imagine being asked to describe a time you led a team through a difficult project. This question assesses leadership skills, decision-making, and collaboration. To prepare, select an experience where you successfully guided a team, focusing on the challenges encountered and the strategies employed to overcome them. Articulate your thought process, the actions taken to motivate and support your team, and the positive outcomes achieved. Practicing this scenario can reinforce your ability to convey leadership qualities effectively.

Consider a scenario where you are asked to discuss a situation in which you had to adapt to a sudden change. This question evaluates resilience and flexibility. Reflect on an experience where you faced unexpected challenges, such as a sudden shift in project priorities or resources. Describe how you assessed the situation, adjusted your approach, and maintained productivity despite the disruption. This practice helps demonstrate your capacity to remain composed and resourceful in the face of change.

Another scenario might involve explaining how you resolved a conflict within a team. Conflict resolution skills are vital in collaborative environments. Think of a time when differing opinions or misunderstandings arose in a group setting. Detail the steps you took to mediate the situation, ensuring open communication and fostering a collaborative atmosphere. Highlight the resolution achieved and any lessons learned. Preparing for this scenario enables you to showcase your ability to navigate interpersonal dynamics effectively.

To simulate a scenario focused on problem-solving, consider being asked about a complex challenge you encountered and how you addressed it. Select an instance where you faced a multifaceted issue requiring critical thinking and innovation. Outline the problem, the options considered, and the rationale behind your chosen solution. Emphasize the positive impact of your actions and any skills demonstrated, such as analytical thinking or creativity. This scenario preparation underscores your problem-solving prowess.

Incorporating feedback into your mock interview practice is crucial for improvement. Conduct these scenarios with peers, mentors, or career counselors who can provide constructive criticism and insights. Their observations can highlight areas where your responses may lack clarity or depth, guiding you toward more effective communication. Constructive feedback also helps identify non-verbal cues to enhance your overall presentation.

Recording your mock interviews offers a valuable opportunity for self-assessment. Reviewing these recordings allows you to evaluate your performance objectively, focusing on aspects such as clarity, pacing, and body language. Take note of any tendencies, such as filler words or unclear explanations, and work to address them in future practice sessions. This self-reflective approach fosters continuous improvement and confidence.

Diversifying the individuals conducting your mock interviews can also be beneficial. Engaging with different interviewers exposes you to varied questioning styles and perspectives, simulating the unpredictability of an actual interview panel. This variety helps build adaptability and prepares you to respond effectively to diverse interview dynamics.

Throughout the mock interview scenarios, emphasize authenticity and sincerity in your responses. The goal is not to recite rehearsed answers but to convey genuine experiences and insights. Authenticity resonates with interviewers, demonstrating your integrity and reliability as a candidate. Focus on articulating your unique strengths and contributions, ensuring your responses reflect your individuality.

In addition to practicing specific scenarios, familiarize yourself with common interview questions and themes. While no two interviews are identical, certain questions frequently arise, such as inquiries about strengths and weaknesses, career goals, or motivations for joining the civil service. Preparing for these common questions ensures you are well-equipped to handle them with confidence.

Finally, use mock interview scenarios to build comfort with the interview process itself. Familiarity with the format and structure reduces anxiety and allows you to approach the actual interview with poise. By practicing under simulated conditions, you create a mental framework that supports calmness and focus during the real interview.

CHAPTER 9

NAVIGATING POST-EXAM OPPORTUNITIES

Interpreting Exam Results

Understanding and interpreting your civil service exam results is a critical step in navigating post-exam opportunities. The results not only reflect your performance but also guide the next steps in your journey toward a career in public service. Analyzing these results with precision and insight can help identify strengths, uncover areas for improvement, and shape future strategies.

When you receive your exam results, the first step is to thoroughly review the score report. This document typically includes your raw scores, percentile rankings, and, in some cases, an analysis of your performance in different sections or competencies. Each component provides valuable information about your overall standing and specific areas of expertise or challenge. Pay close attention to the breakdown of scores, as it reveals where you excelled and where further development might be beneficial.

Your raw score indicates the number of questions answered correctly. While this is a basic measure of performance, it is essential to contextualize it within the broader framework of the exam. Percentile rankings offer a comparative perspective, showing how your performance stacks up against other candidates. A high percentile ranking suggests strong relative performance, indicating competitiveness for roles that require top-tier candidates.

Consider each section of the exam individually, especially if your score report provides a detailed breakdown. This analysis helps pinpoint specific strengths and weaknesses, offering a roadmap for targeted improvement. For instance, if you excelled in analytical reasoning but struggled with verbal communication, this insight can guide your future preparation and focus. Understanding your performance across different competencies is crucial for personal growth and professional development.

Reflect on the connection between your exam results and the competencies required for your desired role. Cross-reference your performance with the job description and requirements to assess alignment. This reflection not only helps in understanding your current suitability for the role but also highlights areas where you may need to enhance your skills or knowledge. The goal is to bridge any gaps between your capabilities and the expectations of the position.

If your results fall short of your expectations or the requirements for a particular role, consider it an opportunity for growth rather than a setback. Analyze the factors that may have contributed to the outcome, such as time management, question interpretation, or test-day conditions. Identifying these factors enables you to develop strategies to address them in future attempts. Embrace a growth mindset, viewing the experience as a learning opportunity that strengthens your resolve and resilience.

Seek feedback and guidance from mentors, peers, or career counselors to gain additional perspectives on your performance. Their insights can provide valuable context and support as you interpret your results and plan your next steps. Engaging with others also opens the door to networking opportunities, which can be instrumental in navigating the post-exam landscape.

Consider enrolling in workshops, courses, or study groups to address areas where improvement is needed. These resources can offer structured learning and practice opportunities, equipping you with the skills and knowledge to enhance your performance in future exams. Additionally, they provide a platform for collaboration and support, fostering connections with fellow candidates who share similar goals.

While interpreting your exam results, it's essential to keep an eye on the bigger picture—your long-term career goals in public service. Use your results as a stepping stone to evaluate your aspirations and the paths available to you. Whether it means pursuing additional training, seeking entry-level positions, or exploring alternative roles that align with your strengths, your exam performance is just one element of your broader career trajectory.

Celebrate your achievements and acknowledge your hard work, regardless of the outcome. The dedication and effort invested in preparing for and taking the civil service exam are commendable accomplishments. Reflecting on this journey fosters a sense of accomplishment and motivation to continue pursuing your career goals.

Establish a plan for next steps based on your interpretation of the results. If you passed the exam and meet the requirements for your desired role, focus on preparing for subsequent stages, such as interviews or assessments. If further improvement is needed, set realistic goals and timelines for addressing identified areas of development. A clear plan provides direction and purpose, ensuring you remain focused and driven in your pursuit of a civil service career.

Stay informed about any changes or updates related to the civil service exam or application process. This awareness ensures you are prepared for future opportunities and can adapt to any evolving requirements or expectations. Being proactive and informed positions you as a knowledgeable and engaged candidate, ready to seize opportunities as they arise.

Building a Career Plan

Crafting a career plan following the civil service exam is a crucial step in transforming your aspirations into actionable goals. This strategic approach enables you to chart a clear path towards a fulfilling career in public service, aligning your skills, interests, and values with opportunities in the field. By considering both short-term and long-term objectives, you can create a roadmap that guides your professional journey with purpose and direction.

Begin by conducting a thorough self-assessment to understand your strengths, weaknesses, and interests. Reflect on the skills and experiences you've acquired during your exam preparation and throughout your educational and professional history. Consider the competencies that were highlighted during the exam and identify areas where you excelled or could improve. This introspection provides a foundation for your career plan, ensuring it is tailored to your unique capabilities and aspirations.

Once you've gained a clear understanding of your skills and interests, explore the various career paths available within the civil service. Research different roles, departments, and specializations to identify positions that align with your strengths and values. Consider the impact you wish to make in public service and the areas where you feel most passionate about contributing. This exploration helps narrow down your options and focus your efforts on roles that resonate with your career goals.

Set specific, measurable, achievable, relevant, and time-bound (SMART) goals for your career. These objectives serve as milestones that guide your progress and keep you motivated. For instance, a short-term goal might be to secure an entry-level position within a year, while a long-term goal could involve advancing to a leadership role within a specific department. By establishing clear goals, you create a framework for your career plan that outlines the steps needed to achieve your aspirations.

Identify the skills and qualifications required for your desired roles and assess any gaps in your current abilities. Develop a plan to acquire these skills through further education, training, or professional development opportunities. Consider enrolling in relevant courses, attending workshops, or seeking mentorship from experienced professionals in your field. This proactive approach ensures you are well-prepared to meet the demands of your desired positions and remain competitive in the job market.

Networking is an essential component of building a successful career plan. Engage with professionals in the civil service through industry events, online platforms, or professional associations. Building relationships with individuals who share your interests and goals can provide valuable insights, support, and opportunities for collaboration. Networking also increases your visibility within the field, opening doors to potential job opportunities and career advancement.

Seek out mentors who can offer guidance and support as you navigate your career path. A mentor's experience and perspective can provide invaluable advice on achieving your goals and overcoming challenges. Establishing a mentorship relationship involves mutual respect and commitment, with both parties benefiting from the exchange of knowledge and experience. A mentor can also introduce you to new opportunities and help expand your professional network.

Stay informed about trends and developments in the civil service sector to ensure your career plan remains relevant and adaptable. Regularly review industry publications, attend conferences, and participate in professional development activities to stay updated on changes and innovations within the field. This awareness allows you to anticipate shifts in the job market and adjust your career plan accordingly, ensuring you remain aligned with the evolving landscape of public service.

Evaluate your progress regularly to ensure you are on track to achieve your goals. Reflect on your accomplishments, assess any areas where you may have deviated from your plan, and make adjustments as necessary. This ongoing evaluation helps maintain focus and motivation, allowing you to celebrate successes and learn from setbacks. Regularly updating your career plan ensures it remains a dynamic tool that supports your growth and development.

Consider alternative pathways or opportunities that may arise along your career journey. While having a structured plan is important, remaining open to new experiences and challenges can lead to unexpected and rewarding opportunities. Flexibility and adaptability are key attributes in navigating the complexities of a public service career, allowing you to seize opportunities that align with your evolving interests and goals.

Balance your professional aspirations with personal well-being and work-life harmony. A successful career plan considers not only the pursuit of professional achievements but also the importance of maintaining a fulfilling and balanced life. Prioritize activities and relationships that contribute to your overall happiness and well-being, ensuring your career complements rather than compromises your personal life.

Exploring Public Service Roles

After the completion of your civil service exam, the world of public service opens up with a myriad of roles that promise both personal fulfillment and professional growth. Exploring these roles requires a strategic approach, understanding the landscape, and aligning your skills with the positions that best suit your aspirations. The journey into public service can be as varied as the individuals who embark on it, with opportunities spanning across local, state, and federal levels.

Embarking on this exploration involves first understanding the structure and function of different government entities. Each level of government offers distinct roles that cater to various public needs and services. On the local level, opportunities often focus on community-based services, including roles in city planning, public health, and local law enforcement. These positions are integral to the daily functioning and improvement of communities, offering a direct impact on citizens' lives.

At the state level, roles expand to include broader policy development, education administration, and infrastructure management. State governments often serve as the bridge between local needs and federal mandates, requiring professionals who can navigate complex regulatory environments and advocate for regional priorities. Positions in state government may involve working closely with legislative bodies, educational institutions, and public works departments.

Federal roles, on the other hand, offer the chance to engage with national and international issues. These positions often involve policy analysis, diplomatic service, and national security, among others. Working at the federal level can provide a platform for influencing large-scale initiatives and reforms, requiring a deep understanding of national and global contexts. The breadth of federal opportunities allows for specialization in areas like environmental policy, economic development, or defense strategy.

As you explore these roles, consider the specific competencies and qualifications each position demands. Public service roles often require a blend of technical skills, policy knowledge, and interpersonal abilities. For instance, a position in public health might necessitate expertise in health policy and data analysis, while a role in urban planning could require skills in geographic information systems (GIS) and community engagement.

Networking plays a crucial role in navigating public service careers. Connecting with current or former public servants can provide insights into the day-to-day realities of different roles, the challenges faced, and the skills needed to succeed. Attend industry conferences, join professional associations, and engage in online forums to expand your network and learn from the experiences of others. These connections can also lead to mentorship opportunities, offering guidance and support as you transition into a public service career.

Gaining relevant experience through internships or volunteer work can also be invaluable. These opportunities allow you to apply your knowledge in real-world settings, develop practical skills, and demonstrate your commitment to public service. Internships in government agencies or non-profit organizations can provide a foot in the door, leading to future employment opportunities. Volunteering for community projects or advocacy groups can also enhance your understanding of public needs and strengthen your professional profile.

As you consider different roles, reflect on your own values and motivations for pursuing a career in public service. Public service is often driven by a desire to contribute to the greater good, improve society, and make a positive impact on people's lives. Identifying the issues or causes you are passionate about can help guide your exploration and ensure alignment with roles that resonate with your personal mission.

Staying informed about current events and trends in public policy is essential for those aspiring to enter public service. Understanding the challenges and opportunities facing society today enables you to position yourself as an informed and proactive candidate. Follow news outlets, policy journals, and government publications to remain up-to-date on developments that may influence public service roles and priorities.

Consider the potential for career advancement and growth within different public service roles. Many government positions offer clear paths for progression, with opportunities to move into leadership or specialized roles over time. Evaluate the training and development programs available within different agencies, as these can provide valuable opportunities to enhance your skills and advance your career.

Balancing career ambitions with personal well-being is crucial in any professional journey, including public service. The demands of public roles can be significant, requiring resilience, dedication, and a strong sense of purpose. Prioritize self-care, maintain a healthy work-life balance, and seek support when needed to ensure long-term success and satisfaction in your career.

Networking and Professional Growth

Networking is a pivotal element in navigating post-exam opportunities within the civil service landscape. Establishing and nurturing professional relationships can open doors to new possibilities, provide valuable insights, and foster career growth. Understanding the nuances of effective networking and leveraging these connections can significantly enhance your professional trajectory, transforming opportunities into tangible career advancements.

Consider the nature of networking as an ongoing, reciprocal process rather than a one-time event. Building relationships takes time, effort, and genuine interest in others. Approach networking with a mindset of mutual benefit, where both parties contribute to and gain from the relationship. This approach fosters trust and respect, laying the groundwork for enduring professional connections.

Begin by identifying key individuals and groups within the civil service ecosystem who can offer guidance, mentorship, or collaboration opportunities. These may include current or former colleagues, educators, industry professionals, or members of professional organizations. Establishing connections with those who share your interests or career goals can provide a support network that enriches your professional journey.

Engage in industry events, workshops, and conferences to expand your network and stay informed about trends and developments in public service. These events offer a platform to meet like-minded professionals, exchange ideas, and explore potential collaborations. Approach these interactions with curiosity and openness, asking thoughtful questions and actively listening to others' perspectives. This engagement demonstrates your commitment to the field and your willingness to learn from and contribute to the community.

Utilize online platforms to extend your networking efforts beyond geographical boundaries. Professional networking sites, forums, and social media groups enable you to connect with individuals across the globe, broadening your exposure to diverse ideas and opportunities. Be proactive in joining discussions, sharing insights, and offering support to others, building a dynamic online presence that reflects your expertise and interests.

Cultivate relationships with mentors who can provide guidance and support as you navigate your career path. A mentor's experience and perspective can offer invaluable advice on achieving your goals, overcoming challenges, and making informed decisions. Seek mentors who align with your values and aspirations, and be open to their feedback and suggestions. A successful mentorship relationship involves mutual respect, trust, and a willingness to learn and grow together.

Participate in professional associations and organizations related to public service. These groups often host events, webinars, and networking opportunities that allow you to engage with peers and industry leaders. Membership in professional associations also demonstrates your commitment to the field and provides access to resources that can enhance your knowledge and skills.

As you build your network, focus on maintaining and nurturing these relationships over time. Regularly reach out to your connections, offering updates, sharing relevant information, or simply expressing gratitude for their support. Consistent communication reinforces the bond and ensures your relationships remain active and meaningful. Remember that networking is a two-way street; be willing to offer assistance and support to others when needed.

Leverage your network to seek out opportunities for professional growth and development. Whether it's exploring job openings, gaining insights into industry trends, or identifying potential collaborators for projects, your connections can serve as valuable resources. Be open to new possibilities that arise through your network, and consider how each opportunity aligns with your career goals and aspirations.

Continuous Skill Development

In the ever-evolving realm of public service, continuous skill development stands as a cornerstone for career advancement and personal growth. After navigating the demanding process of civil service exams, successful candidates are faced with the realization that learning does not end at the point of entry. Rather, it is a lifelong journey that ensures relevance, adaptability, and competence in a dynamic professional environment.

The significance of continuous learning is underscored by the rapid changes in technology, policy, and societal needs. As public servants, individuals are tasked with addressing complex challenges that require innovative solutions and a comprehensive understanding of emerging trends. Therefore, embracing a mindset of lifelong learning becomes not merely an option, but a necessity for those seeking to excel in their roles and make meaningful contributions to society.

To begin with, identifying areas for skill enhancement is crucial. Reflect on your current skill set and assess it against the requirements of your role and the broader goals of your department or agency. This self-assessment helps pinpoint specific competencies that need refining or expansion. It can be beneficial to seek feedback from supervisors or colleagues, gaining insights into your strengths and areas for improvement. This feedback serves as a valuable tool for guiding your learning journey.

Once you've identified areas for growth, explore various avenues for skill development. Formal education programs, such as advanced degrees or certifications, offer structured learning experiences that can deepen your expertise in specific areas. Enrolling in courses related to public policy, data analysis, or management can enhance your ability to tackle complex tasks and lead initiatives effectively. These programs not only expand your knowledge but also often provide networking opportunities with professionals in similar fields.

In addition to formal education, consider engaging in workshops, seminars, or conferences that focus on current trends and challenges in public service. These events offer insights into industry best practices, innovative solutions, and emerging technologies. Participating in discussions and workshops allows you to exchange ideas with peers and experts, fostering a culture of collaborative learning and innovation.

Online learning platforms have become increasingly popular and accessible, providing a flexible and cost-effective way to acquire new skills. From short courses to comprehensive programs, these platforms cover a wide range of subjects pertinent to public service. Whether it's honing your communication skills, mastering data visualization tools, or understanding the nuances of public finance, online courses offer the convenience of learning at your own pace, tailored to your specific needs.

Mentorship is another invaluable component of continuous skill development. Establishing a relationship with a mentor who has extensive experience in public service can provide guidance, support, and encouragement as you navigate your career. A mentor can offer practical advice, share personal experiences, and help you develop the skills necessary to achieve your professional goals. This relationship is mutually beneficial, as mentors often gain fresh perspectives and renewed motivation from their mentees.

Furthermore, consider the power of experiential learning. On-the-job experiences, special projects, and cross-departmental initiatives present opportunities to apply new skills in real-world settings. Taking on challenging assignments or leadership roles can stretch your capabilities and build confidence. These experiences not only solidify your learning but also demonstrate your commitment to personal and professional growth, enhancing your reputation as a proactive and resourceful public servant.

Engaging in reflective practices is an often-overlooked aspect of skill development. Regularly reflecting on your experiences, successes, and setbacks provides deeper insights into your learning process. Journaling, self-assessment, or peer discussions can help you identify patterns, recognize achievements, and plan for future growth. This reflective practice fosters self-awareness and adaptability, key attributes for thriving in a public service career.

Collaborative learning is a powerful tool for skill development, as it encourages the sharing of knowledge and experiences among peers. Establish or join a study group or professional network where members can discuss challenges, share resources, and support each other's growth. This collective approach not only enhances learning but also builds a sense of community and camaraderie among public servants.

Keep abreast of technological advancements that impact public service. Familiarity with digital tools and platforms, such as data analytics software, project management applications, and communication technologies, is essential for modern public service roles. Developing technical proficiency can enhance your efficiency, effectiveness, and ability to innovate in your work.

Lastly, cultivate a growth mindset, the belief that abilities and intelligence can be developed through dedication and hard work. This mindset fosters a love for learning and resilience in the face of challenges. Embrace failures and setbacks as opportunities for growth and learning, understanding that they are part of the journey toward mastery and excellence.

EXTRA CONTENTS

Audiobook

Listen to the book's content while you're on the go. It's perfect for absorbing information without needing to read, ideal if you're short on time.

Digital Flashcards

Easily review key concepts with digital flashcards. They're quick to use and help you reinforce information wherever you are.

+200 Terms For Civil Service

You'll find over 200 terms that will help you better understand exam questions and approach the test with more confidence.

Foreign Education Evaluation Guide

This guide walks you through the steps and offices you need to contact to get your foreign educational qualifications evaluated.

Sites To Candidate For Each State

A list of websites where you can apply for Civil Service positions in each state, saving you time and making the process faster.

Click or scan the QR CODE below and access the bonuses

https://civilservice.newpublishingagency.com/step-1-page-2176-4756-6529-1613-9417

Made in the USA
Las Vegas, NV
31 October 2024